PRAISE FOR *THE BEST IS YET TO COME*

This book is about finding hope against all odds, even in the darkest of situations. We all face pain, disappointments, heartaches and struggles in life that can sometimes lead down a seemingly hopeless path of deep devastation; yet Tara shows us there is always hope. Through brave and inspiring honesty about her own difficult personal experiences, she shows us that hope is always within our grasp if we make the choice to embrace it and that, no matter our situation, the best really can be yet to come.

Ivan Misner, PhD,
NY Times bestselling author and founder of BNI®

When the doctors place paddles on your heart they do it to shock you back to life. Sometimes, that is exactly what we need spiritually—a shock back to reality.

Grieving is healthy, but wallowing in remorse and regret is hurtful—to yourself. This book will lovingly and gently shock you back toward wholeness with one simple and seldom used technique... HONESTY.

Tara gracefully walks you through her pain and shows you how to find the BLESS in any mess so you can graciously let go of the hurt and gratefully move toward healing.

Barry Spilchuk,
author of *THE cANCER DANCE*

When a relationship finds its genesis in God and is based on a three-way relationship with God in the middle, death provides a temporary interruption, but no more than that. For here is a story of the love between two people that is only waiting for its final reunion… and that part of this story remains on hold.

Rev. Dr. Clive Calver,
Senior Pastor of Walnut Hill Community Church, Connecticut, and former president of World Relief

The Best is Yet to Come is an inspiring masterpiece. Its message will give you a whole new perspective on God's plan for your life. Tara is a remarkable writer and a gripping storyteller who will keep you enthralled to the very last page.

Arvee Robinson,
The Master Speaker Trainer,
international speaker and author

Inspiring! Tara uncovers how one can trust God and self in the face of real testing. Through her story, she illustrates how we each can overcome the difficulties in our lives and come out stronger in the end.

David Horsager,
bestselling author of *The Trust Edge*

Through *The Best is Yet to Come,* Tara reminds us that God often says "yes" and we take it for granted. Sometimes, God says "no" because he knows what we are asking for is not in the best interest of those affected. It is at these times when the child in us asks "Why not?" The book flows from the life of the author with wonderful anecdotes of the joy of meeting Frank and the emotions that followed.

Dr. Michael C. Redmond, PhD,
psychoneurologist, reverend, speaker and author of
How To Be Happy and Master Your Work Life Balance

Tara shows us through her story how to avoid turning against God during trials, but to keep Him on our side—trusting that He ultimately knows what is best for us.

Haley Hatch Freeman,
professional speaker and author of
A Future for Tomorrow: Surviving Anorexia, My Spiritual Journey

The Best is Yet to Come is delightful, then heartbreaking, then inspiring, in its portrayal of the revelations a sovereign God uses to demonstrate His love, both in and for Tara and Frank.

It is the true story of how a quirk leads to serendipity, and ultimately turns out to be an unexpected grace! An overlooked "feature" in an email program starts a relationship that only God could use to bring the joy, comfort and reassurance of His presence in the lives of two people who might not have found it on their own.

Yes, I will admit that halfway through the book I was shaking my head, asking "How could You do this? You're supposed to be a loving Father!" But by the time Tara finishes telling their story, I'm drawn even closer to Him, and I think you will be too!

By all means, read and share this wonderful story!

Howard J. Tuckey,
author of *Mattie's Place*

Tara R. Alemany systematically communicates spiritual strength and mental discipline as she fueled and guided me from heart to head and back again. I am forever grateful to her for sharing her open-hearted journey embracing the magic and mystery of self-love, love of another, and God's love.

Carol Metz Murray,
transformational change agent,
speaker and business consultant

Also by Tara R. Alemany

Christian Nonfiction
My Love to You Always
Celebrating 365 Days of Gratitude (13th ed.)

Business Leadership
The Character-Based Leader
80 Easy Ways to Supercharge Your Business Growth

Authorship
The Plan that Launched a Thousand Books
Publish with Purpose

The Best is Yet to Come

The Best is Yet to Come

by
TARA R. ALEMANY

EMERALD LAKE
BOOKS
Sherman, Connecticut

The Best is Yet To Come
Copyright © 2021 Tara Alemany

Cover design by Mark Gerber
Cover illustration copyright © 2021 Mark Gerber

All rights reserved. No part of this book may be used or reproduced by any means, graphic, electronic or mechanical, including photocopying, recording, taping or by any information storage retrieval system, without the written permission of the publisher except in the case of brief quotations embodied in critical articles and reviews.

The Best is Yet to Come refers to actual people and events. Events, locales and conversations have been reconstructed with as much accuracy and detail as possible. In order to maintain their anonymity, in some instances, the names of individuals and places have been changed.

The email excerpts throughout the book are actual quotations, shared without alteration.

Books published by Emerald Lake Books may be ordered through your favorite booksellers or by visiting emeraldlakebooks.com.

ISBN: 978-1-945847-39-4 (paperback)
        978-1-945847-38-7 (hardcover)
        978-1-945847-40-0 (ebook)
        978-1-945847-43-1 (large print)

Library of Congress Control Number: 2021931036

CONTENTS

Prologue	xv
Surprised by Frank	1
The Open Door	7
Past Experiences	9
The List	13
Ongoing Pain	17
Negotiations	21
The Object of His Desire	25
The Simple Things	29
Beaten by a Girl	31
Spiritual Warfare Begins	33
Growing Together	37
Blending Families	41
Working Together	45
Dueling Poems	49
The Gift of Dirt	53
Praying on Our Knees	55
Studying the Word	61
The Test of a Relationship	63
Too Much Quiet	67
Hope Arises and Then Swan Dives	71
Finding the Courage to Call	73

The Awful News 75
A Storm Within and a Storm Without 79
In the Aftermath of Alfred 83
Calling Papa Frank 87
Identifying Frank 91
Making Arrangements 95
The Best is Yet to Come 99
A Protective Family 105
My Breakfast Meeting 109
The Funeral 115
Meeting Papa Frank 121
The Service in the Village 125
An Eternal Love 129
A New Beginning for Grasshopper 131
In the Valley 137
The Irony of Pain 139
The Gift Frank Left Behind 145
A New Beginning 147
Author's Note 153
Discussion Guide 159
Acknowledgments 165
About the Author 169

DEDICATION

This book is dedicated to anyone who has stood at a crossroads with a friend and waited patiently with them as they decided which way to turn.

Mark Gerber, you've been that person for me. Your friendship means more to me than I can say. Your steady, kind and gentle presence helped a broken heart to heal and a spirit to dream again. My life would have been much emptier without your support and encouragement. Thank you for being there for me and believing in me, even when I doubted myself. Without you, this story would have been incomplete.

I'm a success today because I had
a friend who believed in me and I didn't
have the heart to let him down.
~ Abe Lincoln

PROLOGUE

Have you ever experienced a situation where life as you knew it completely changed? That's the position I found myself in during the latter half of 2011. Over the course of four short months, my life went from stable, uninteresting, mundane, but secure, through the roller coaster ride of new love to the devastating effects of unexpected loss.

This is my story. It's a love story set in the Internet Age, but what love story isn't these days? More importantly, this story reflects how God still moves in the world, even when we struggle with what He is doing.

Perhaps for you the name "God" has too much religion associated with it. Please don't let that stop you from reading this book. If, for your own comfort, you want to substitute "God" with "the Universe" or "Life" or whatever else it is that you believe in, feel free to do so. The lessons shared here are universal. They are part of the human condition when living with loss.

I refer to the time that began with these events as my "year without walls." I'm not talking about physical walls, but the mental and emotional ones we erect to keep ourselves safe. As you journey through this story with me, I'll share the lessons I learned and the incredible blessing that comes from truly connecting with others without the hindrance of barriers.

These lessons don't just apply to those mourning the loss of a loved one. Grief comes in many shapes and forms. You may be mourning the loss of a job, a career, a home, a marriage, a business, a dream or any number of the other setbacks of life.

Hopefully, as you read my story, you'll start to see how simple changes in perspective can help you take a devastating loss and turn it into the foundation of something new and powerful in your life. As Vivian Greene is quoted as saying, "Life's not about waiting for the storm to pass… It's about learning to dance in the rain!"

I look forward to sharing the journey with you.

Tara R. Alemany
Sherman, Connecticut
January 14, 2013

SURPRISED BY FRANK

Within a few short days, it became difficult to tell where he left off and I began. I wasn't looking for love anymore. I thought for sure those days had passed me by. Then, I was surprised by Frank.

Our time together became a microcosm of the life we wanted to have, running at full speed.

It's hard to say where it all began, but I *can* pinpoint a specific series of events that was clear and obvious. So that's where I'll start.

There's an online group in the area where I live called "ReUseIt." The ReUseIt Network helps get material goods from people who have them, but don't want them, to people who want them, but don't have them. Simple enough…

I had an old broken-down push mower. It was beyond repair, but could potentially be used for parts or a student project. Before taking it to the dump, I wanted to see if anyone might want it, so I sent an email to the group with the specifics about the mower.

Part of the group's guidelines dictate that you can't include links or attachments in any posts you share. This protects the membership from viruses and unsafe or unexpected content.

Now, let me tell you a little bit about the email system I used… It's inexpensive. As such, it reserved the right to do things I don't necessarily like, but never thought twice about before. For example, when I pressed the Send button, it added a little three-line, text advertisement to the bottom of my note. Invariably, one of those lines is a link to further information, but because it's added after I send the note, I never saw it.

So, when I posted my offer on July 1, 2011, I was completely surprised to see it rejected on July 2! The moderator of the group, Frank, sent me the guidelines for using the site, prefaced by a two-word reason for the rejection. *NO LINKS!*

I actually had to scroll through the note several times before I even saw it buried in with all of the other text. I couldn't figure out why I'd been sent the guidelines at all. At first, that's all I saw.

I knew there was no way my response would be as short as his direction, and he'd kindly provided his phone number in his signature. I considered writing my reply, but realized it would take significantly longer to explain that way, and it seemed like a two-minute phone conversation would easily resolve the issue. While I'm not a "phone person," I picked up the phone, dialed the number, and proceeded to introduce myself to the man on the other end of the line.

I explained the situation to him. He politely explained the rules of the group to me one more time, just in case I didn't understand them from the email. Then he agreed to remove the link himself this time, but warned me not to let it happen again.

Conversation over, right? Wrong!

Somehow in the few minutes we spoke, he picked up on a detail or two about me, and he wanted to learn more. The questions were innocent enough, but led to more things to discuss.

What I thought would be a two-minute conversation ended up lasting an hour. So much for brevity... But on a Saturday afternoon, I had the time to spare, and I sensed he was lonely. I thought I was just being kind by allowing the conversation to take its course. After twenty minutes or so though, I started to realize, *This guy is kind of neat. He's got a great sense of humor. He's intelligent. I like the way his mind works. We have a lot of interests in common.*

We talked about movies, his dogs (Falcore and Bear), my cat (Brody), places we'd been, careers we'd had, and so many other things. I told him about being a martial artist and pursuing my black belt in the coming spring.

He was trying to remember an actor's name, but couldn't. So, he finished stating that he was sure he'd remember it at 3:30 in the morning, and he'd let me know. I joked that he really didn't need to, as I expected I'd be sleeping then.

The next morning, I awoke to an email from him. The subject line of the email was "Promised 0330 announcement," and it started "Hey, Grasshopper" (a nod to the nickname David Carradine's teacher gave his character in the 1970s television show *Kung Fu*).

The note provided the promised missing name, touched on some of the things we'd talked about the day before, and ended with:

> I really enjoyed talking with you today—you made my day,,,,,Falcore is indifferent to the cat, but Bear wants to know more. Does she cuddle? Cook? Date older men (he's 3 ½).

Falcore is female, and Bear is male, as is my cat, Brody. In my response to his inquiries, I ended with:

> Bear may be disappointed to learn that the cat is older than he is, and is a boy. Brody is about 4.5 years old now, and is a sweetheart. Yes, he enjoys cuddling. Last I knew, cats don't find cooking necessary, although he does have a discerning palate.
>
> If Bear's questions are a veiled method of learning more about me, well… I'm not dating and haven't been for the

past twelve years. While I've been busy raising my kids and earning a living, it's not just that. Fourteen years ago (in August), I was born again in Christ. My one and only dating relationship as a Christian didn't quite go how I'd hoped, and I realized I needed to take some time and figure things out first. Things like, what does a dating relationship look like in the context of a Christian faith compared to the way I'd been doing things all my life prior to that? I also realized I needed time to straighten things out in my heart and mind regarding past failed relationships. That time gave me the opportunity as well to identify what it is I want out of a relationship and what qualities were key to find in a potential partner, which certainly takes a lot of heartache out of dating. I won't go out with someone unless I've already seen some of the key qualities displayed.

I quickly figured out that one thing that was lacking in most of my past connections was friendship. So, I'm not jumping into dating anyone, although I am open to getting to know people. (I even have a profile on a Christian dating site, although little has come from it.)

For the most part, I consider age to be simply a number. I have friends spanning from 100 years old to friends who are still in their teens. But my ex-husband is significantly older than I am, and thus left a bad impression of dating older men. I'm open to God's leading in my life, trusting He knows the perfect person for me (not a perfect person, but The One He made with me in mind). If he turns out to be older, so be it! I'm okay with that. The only way I'll recognize it though is to get to know him as a person (not in the context of romance). I know what I want in the last man I give my heart to, and I know what God wants for me. So, I think I'll recognize him when the time comes.

If Bear really wasn't interested in all that, you don't have to read it to him. :-)

I expected that my response was closing a door. Little did I know, it was the key to opening his heart!

THE OPEN DOOR

Having been "found out," Frank admitted readily enough that Bear wasn't really the one interested in learning more. Frank was "quite taken with our conversation," and with me. His responding email said as much and continued the multiple points of conversation we had running at the time.

While we hadn't spoken about faith at all until I made my bold declaration, he told me about his experience being born again at the age of twelve, the church he was raised in, the Christian community he lived in now, and how he had studied to be a minister when he went to college causing a rift between him and his father. Unfortunately, mid-way through the program, the college dropped his five-year degree program, meaning he'd have to complete a four-year program followed by four years of seminary. As he put it:

YIKES! TME=too much schooling-I mean education.

More importantly to me, he told me that, except for a month-long relationship five years earlier, he'd been alone himself for ten years and that more than anything he wanted to meet a Christian Gal and let the Lord lead to where that lady and he would serve. I found it ironic that he used the phrase "Christian Gal" because that happened to be my profile name on the dating site I used—ChristianGal817.

This whole revelation was just the first of many such "God-incidences," as a friend used to call them. But at the time, it seemed simply incredible, and I wasn't certain what to make of it.

That same day, the 4th of July, Frank called me for the first time. I had company at the time and was surprised, thrilled and embarrassed he'd called, all at the same time. Speaking on the kitchen phone with my mother standing nearby, I quickly informed him that I had company and asked if it was possible for him to call again later that evening. He said he just wanted to let me know how much he was enjoying talking with me, and he'd be happy to call later. As I hung up the phone and my mother looked questioningly at me, all I could come up with to say was, "It seems I have a secret admirer." I can't remember the last time I had blushed prior to that, but I know for certain I did then!

PAST EXPERIENCES

As Frank and I wrote back and forth, we shared our experiences using online dating sites, talked about our educational backgrounds, and expounded on the movies we loved (or didn't).

My profile had been on a Christian dating site and had yielded three poor matches for me.

The first guy was someone who, after a few weeks of chatting, called me one day in a panic. He told me he was going to be homeless soon unless he could raise $30K to pay off a gambling debt and could I help him? When I didn't, he disappeared, never to be heard from again.

The second was someone local, who invited me out for a cup of coffee. We met, and he admitted right away that he was a convicted sex offender who had served his time and was trying to rebuild his life. While I appreciated his candor, my own personal experiences as the victim of child molestation and eventually rape meant I really couldn't see a connection developing there. It was just too unsettling.

The third guy had promise. We got along well, enjoyed talking with each other, and finally decided to meet. While that was all good, an issue started to rapidly develop. At that point, I'd been alone about ten years, having never shared parenting duties with anyone else, and was just trying to feel my way through what a relationship could or should be like. However, his biological clock was ticking!

He had no children of his own and really wanted some. His hope was to get married within six months to a year, and my current age meant six months was preferable. It became quickly apparent that his needs and mine just didn't mesh together. He did eventually go on to meet someone else who seemed more promising, and I was happy to see him move on.

For Frank, he'd had conversations with people and made friends, but never found that person who challenged and engaged him, which was something important to him. He wanted someone he could build a life with, find a place to serve together, and who enjoyed his sense of humor, which he believed was his finest quality. He also wanted someone who could keep up with him intellectually and would understand his more esoteric references; things like the fact that one of his dogs was named for the flying dragon in The NeverEnding Story.

It was important to him to know what I was looking for in a man, and I appreciated the opportunity to share. One of the primary reasons I hadn't entered into any relationships was because I was very clear on what I was looking for. He had to be a Christian guy. That was non-negotiable.

Age wasn't as big a factor for me as it might be for others. All of my relationships have been with "older guys;" the closest in age to me being seven years older. The majority of my relationships were with men who were twelve to fifteen years my senior.

Ultimately, I discovered Frank was seventeen years older than me. While I recognized it meant I'd most likely spend my latter years alone if things worked out between us, it was okay for now. My grandfather and his wife had also been seventeen years apart in age. Yet, they built a wonderful life together. When he died, a new companion did enter her life, and there was always that hope for me as well.

So, our age difference was not a show-stopper for me. However, past experience had taught me to be cautious when I entered a relationship, to be sure we both *truly* wanted the same things out of life.

THE LIST

I already knew what I was looking for in my ideal partner. Eleven years earlier, a friend of mine and I were talking about relationships. Nigel had found "The One" and was preparing to marry her. I was wrestling with the bad choices I'd made in the past and the dysfunctional model I'd had as a kid growing up.

That had led me to years of "trying on" relationships to see what might fit, with no consideration as to whether that person or relationship was actually a good match for me. It was like putting together a puzzle blindfolded, with no regard for the pattern of the picture, randomly picking up pieces to see if they fit and hoping there was a way to mash them together.

I asked my friend how I would know the right person when I found him if I really didn't have a solid track record in that area. Nigel recommended I spend some time in prayer and reflection and then write a list of those qualities God would have included in the man He created especially for me. Knowing myself and that God desired a happy, Christ-centered relationship for me, what were the qualities my significant other would need to display to be my ideal mate?

That made sense to me. It was like finally taking the blindfold off while working on the puzzle. Now patterns, colors, shapes and sizes all played a role in finding the pieces that fit.

So, I made my list, coming up with the qualities I felt a prospective partner needed to have based on my own circumstances, past experiences, desires and needs. He needed to be:

- A man of strong Christian faith.
- Someone who valued honor and integrity.
- A man who would do what is right, even when it's hard.
- Someone who understood what it meant to protect his family, and who was willing to lay down his life for them; not just in big ways, but small ones too.
- A man who would share the daily chores and challenges with me.
- Someone caring and compassionate.
- A man with the intellectual capacity to challenge me.
- Someone who understood and embraced the fact I was a package deal.
- A man who could communicate his thoughts and feelings.
- Someone with whom I could disagree and even argue with, yet still feel safe, loved and secure.

This list has saved me a lot of heartache over the years. As I met new people, I could assess them against these qualities. I hate to admit, in the intervening years, I'd only met a few single men who demonstrated more than a handful of them. Yet, each quality was important to me, so I never let those relationships develop beyond friendships.

Within the first three weeks of our meeting, Frank demonstrated every single quality I'd been looking for in a man. Thankfully, in that same three-week period, he realized he couldn't live without me.

Digging Deeper...

When you've wanted something very important in your life, how much time have you spent thinking about and visualizing what it is you want? I mean really getting clear about what it is that would make you happy?

I'm not saying you can simply will something into being. But I do believe there's great opportunity in knowing what you want clearly enough that you can articulate it to another human being. This allows you to recognize it when you see it. It's how you'll actually know when you've found or accomplished what you set out to do!

It's like leaving the house in your car and knowing you want to go buy food. If you haven't decided first whether you'd like to go to a restaurant or a grocery store, you may be heading out too early. And if you've decided you want to go to a restaurant, you may end up eating Italian when you really wanted Chinese, if you're not specific about your choice of restaurant.

The more clearly you can define what it is you want in life, whether in a partner, a job, a home, a family, or anything else, the more likely it is you'll create what you want.

So, I encourage you to get really specific. What is it you want out of life? Out of relationships? Out of opportunities? And, just as important, what is it you don't want?

ONGOING PAIN

Frank had been suffering from diabetes-induced neuropathy for years by the time we met. Most days were spent trying to find a way to get comfortable and ease the pain.

Sometimes, the only resort was to go back to bed. This meant he kept odd hours, often sleeping much of the day, and staying awake throughout the night.

For someone who had spent much of his career as an auxiliary state police officer as well as a first aid and CPR instructor for the American Red Cross, the limitations imposed by his illness were challenging for him to accept.

Although Frank was technically a resident of a nearby town in Connecticut, he'd been living in Florida for the past couple of years. He'd gone down there temporarily with the intent of helping his father recover from an injury. Yet, his constant pain made him unable to help and irritable at times as well.

Once down there, he found it hard to gather his belongings and head back home. He had this idealized notion of how being there to help his father would restore their relationship, but his father had suffered years of disappointments where Frank was concerned and had learned to rely on others in the meantime.

Frank felt, rightfully so, replaced. He had been replaced, but not with the intent of hurting his feelings. His father had found people he could rely upon to help him because he knew Frank was dealing with his own issues and was unreliable as a result. There was no condemnation in it. His father was dealing with the simple facts. Over time, I learned to accept the same thing about Frank. His illness made him unreliable at times. That's not how he wanted to be, but it's the way things turned out.

He had a big heart and the best of intentions but often fell short of his promises. Despite that fact, I came to love him deeply.

I think that's one reason why our long-distance relationship worked so well for him. He was basically house-bound and didn't have to worry about being on time to meet me somewhere. He simply had to answer the phone when I called. Given that he rarely went anywhere, and certainly never without telling me about it first, it was easy for us to connect.

When we weren't on the phone together, he'd watch his NASCAR races, work on his computer, or play with his dogs.

Often though, his day didn't go as planned. This gave birth to his favorite saying. "If I had a plan for today... this would not have been on it." Another sign of that quirky sense of humor I came to love.

One day, when his computer was acting up, he wrote to tell me "MY COMPUTER IS LEARNING German.... it's on the Fritz."

He'd often complain about technology rebelling against him. With the neuropathy in his hands, he struggled with the keyboards of his computer and phone; accidentally turning the caps lock on, fat-fingering typos, etc. But he always took it in stride, acknowledging the problem, wishing it was different, but accepting things were the way they were, and there wasn't a lot he could do but grin and bear it.

Digging Deeper…

Have you ever held so tightly to an outcome you wanted, only to be blind to the blessings in how everything turned out?

Perhaps you were really upset about being passed over for a job promotion. However, if you'd gotten that promotion, you'd have missed half of your daughter's dance recitals or your son's baseball games in the past year alone.

Or perhaps the divorce you didn't ask for has left you feeling lost and alone. Yet, this is a fantastic time to rediscover the gifts and talents you've left dormant all of these years while you were struggling to make your marriage work.

Sometimes, the pain we endure is based purely on our inability or unwillingness to look at the situation another way. We stay focused on the outcome we wanted, refusing to let it go, rather than focusing on the potential in how things turned out.

Frank really wanted to be there for his father when he needed help, and he was hurt when his father needed to rely on someone else. He let that disappointment stand in the way of their relationship.

In the end, they never had a chance to reconcile. However, he could have chosen to be happy his father had someone else he could rely upon. The choice truly was his to make.

It's not to say his disappointment wasn't justified, but fueling disappointment doesn't help anyone. It's much healthier to acknowledge it and let it go.

When you've done your best to create the life you want and there's nothing more you can do, it's time to accept the things that are truly beyond your control.

NEGOTIATIONS

Frank sent me a copy of his dating profile from a website, in which I read that he smoked socially. I know so few people who smoke anymore that I find it repellent when I am around someone who does. The odor lingers in hair and clothes, and it isn't easy to mask or cover. So, one of the things important to me in a partner was that they didn't smoke. It hadn't even occurred to me to include "non-smoking" on my list because it seemed such a given to me.

As we discussed it, Frank told me he smoked a pipe but only on occasion (usually when he was driving long distance as a means of biding time). Based on that, he said he'd consider giving it up, but only if I did something for him too.

You see, when he saw my online dating profile, he figured he knew the exact reason why I'd had so few responses to it. He hemmed and hawed about sharing his theory with me, telling me he didn't want me "fixing it" and then someone else trying to steal me away. But, in his opinion, my hair was much too short and made me look like a man.

So, he asked me to grow it out. Initially, I told him "no." I'd had long hair down to the small of my back until my firstborn was about six months old. She'd been pulling it out, a strand at a time, with her gooey little fingers while she was teething. So, to solve my problem, I cut my hair short. The gooey fingers remained, but the hair-pulling stopped quickly.

It had remained the same length for over thirteen years, and I really couldn't see any reason to go back to having to "deal with" longer hair.

But, when discussed in the context of negotiating his stopping smoking, it was something I was willing to consider. Over time, I did grow it out, although not quickly enough for him.

Each time I went for a haircut, I had my stylist take before and after pictures so he could see where we were at and provide input. Of course, it didn't grow fast enough for his liking, and he'd teasingly give me a hard time about it. But it just became another of those shared "inside" joking arguments we'd resort to affectionately.

Frank was never a very patient man when it came to the things he wanted the most. Like a kid waiting for Christmas, time couldn't move fast enough. Add to that the fact that he lived in a world where things were ideally one way or another, and wishy-washy grey spots bothered him. He liked the stark contrast of a black-and-white world and didn't always understand why it wasn't that easy for others.

So, it was hard for him sometimes to accept things weren't always going to go as he hoped. But I had no issue reminding him the world didn't revolve around him, even though mine quickly did.

Digging Deeper...

Do you remember when you were little being taught about sharing and being nice to each other? Our parents and teachers were laying the foundation for learning how to compromise.

Some of us "got" the lesson more easily. It comes naturally to us to think about what another person might want or enjoy. Others of us might find it harder to compromise.

How poorly or well you compromise, though, has a lasting effect on the quality of your life. This is true in business, on a sports team, in a marriage, and in so many other scenarios in life.

The heart of compromise is being able to care enough about someone else to put their needs before your own. Yet, for it to truly work, both parties must be willing to do the same. I put your needs first, while you put mine, and somewhere in the middle is a compromise we both can live with.

It's important to realize though that not all things need to be subject to compromise. We pick and choose those things that, for us, are non-negotiables. Although I'd considered the length of my hair to be non-negotiable, when it was put up against something I cared even more about, it was easy to compromise on.

And the funny thing is... Frank was right. I do look better with longer hair.

THE OBJECT OF HIS DESIRE

The dating profile Frank had sent to me reflected his sense of humor. In it, he described himself as "elevationally challenged," being too short for his weight. While it's a humorous statement on its own, it becomes even more ridiculous when you learn he was a quarter-inch shy of 6′ tall. (And jealous of that quarter inch! He'd always wanted to be 6′ and never quite made it there.)

He also claimed to be too young for his chronological age, since he looked much younger than his sixty years and acted younger too.

The thing that stood out for me in the profile was the way he closed it.

> About the one I'm looking for…
>
> I'm looking for my LAST relationship. I want a long-term relationship with the right woman. I'm not looking for someone I CAN live with—I'm lQQking for someone I CAN'T Live WITHOUT.

As our relationship evolved and deepened, those words kept ringing in my head. Here was someone who wasn't just eager for companionship. He wanted the deep and abiding love that comes from cherishing another.

By the end of our first week of conversations, we were spending a few hours a day on the phone together, and he would tell me "I'm enjoying you so much." I couldn't remember the last time someone had simply enjoyed... me. Not what I did for them. Not how I made them feel. Just the simple fact of my presence... After so many years of feeling like "an odd duck," with Frank, I began to feel that my heart had finally found a home.

The first time he told me "I adore you," I had no idea how to take it. At first, I was disappointed because it seemed a step lower than "I love you," which is what I wanted to hear. Over time, I came to realize how much more encompassing and specific his choice of words was.

Not that I wanted to be put on a pedestal, and he never did that, but to be adored by someone... He was declaring his willingness to put my needs over his; to cherish me and care about the people and things that were important to me. He wasn't using the easily misconstrued word "love." He was being specific.

He didn't just love me. He wanted me. He wanted to be near me. He wanted to be with me. He wanted to share in my daily life, my work, and my world. He reminded me frequently that he wasn't just looking for someone he could live with. He told me:

> I want you, because you're someone I can't live WITHOUT... Just knowing that you are there is heartwarming, and relieving. I don't feel so alone anymore.

I came to realize that "I adore you" was love with an extra-special bit to it, much like when I'd tell my kids "I love you to the moon and back," and we'd go back and forth topping each other to show how much we cared for each other.

As was Frank's nature, he went from 0 to 60 in no time at all. No measly "I love you" from him. He adored me, and I believed him.

He'd do little things all the time just to show me. We'd hang up the phone in the wee hours of the morning so I could get some sleep before having to get up and put the kids on the bus. No sooner would we hang up than he'd be on his computer, sending me an email so it would be waiting there for me in the morning when I awoke. Things like:

> Just wanted to bring a smile to your groggy face. Even if I'm asleep, I'm still thinking about you.

It became a game for us. Sometimes, after we'd hang up the phone, I'd hop on the computer to send him a quick note to see if I could beat him. So, then, he started sending me multiple messages, leaving me a few to find the next time I was online. When it came right down to it, he was a big softie who wore his heart on his sleeve and who liked to pretend he was gruff.

He was always saddling me with new nicknames, so I had to add a few of my own along the way. Over time, he became my "melting curmudgeon" (or "MC," for short) since he pretended to be stern one moment and was characteristically mushy the next.

Digging Deeper...

Are you clear in your language with others? When you express your thoughts, feelings and desires, does the person you're speaking to truly understand what you're sharing?

Sometimes, the English language can be so nebulous. "Love" has so many different shades of meaning that it's almost impossible to understand when it's used out of context.

Add to that the fact that we often mistake one thing for another (for example, lust for love), and it just makes everything all the more confusing.

Yet, communication is key to being able to know and understand one another.

That's why it's important to make every effort to ensure your listener gets your meaning. Making the effort to share isn't enough. Check back with the person you're talking with. Do they understand what you're saying?

That's where our word choices become important too. Think about how your listener communicates. If you're trying to share your feelings with others about something you've experienced in your life, but don't give them some context for understanding (using examples they'd connect with), they won't understand no matter how much they want to. They haven't experienced your exact situation themselves. So, only you can narrate it for them.

Not everyone will care enough to try to understand, but those who do are worth the effort on your part.

THE SIMPLE THINGS

One evening early in July, a friend of my daughter's was on a popular television game show. Frank had heard us talking about Tony's appearance and how there was going to be a showing at Tony's house the evening it aired. While my daughter attended the party, I went back to our house and watched the episode with Frank on the phone, while he watched it on TV at his house.

It was the only time we watched television together, but it was fun doing something so simple and mundane with each other.

As time went on and our relationship deepened, he kept me company as I cooked, worked in the yard, drove to business meetings, took my son to tutoring, bought school clothes for my kids, did the laundry, paid the bills, etc. He wanted to be a part of every facet of my life. We even worked on some of my client projects together.

I had a logo to design for a nonprofit I was on the board of directors for, and Frank provided his two cents at each stage of the process. Since he'd worked in and around the printing industry when he was younger, he was able to make relevant contributions to the project, and I was happy to share the work with him.

Long before Frank turned my world upside down, I'd committed to co-author a book with a community of individuals I'd met on Twitter. It was to be published by a nonprofit as a means of advancing their cause and bringing visibility to their work.

Twenty-one community members had each committed to writing a chapter of the book, which was about character-based leadership. We were asked to write about a characteristic or trait we believed was critical to character-based leadership. I opted to write about perseverance.

This has been a theme throughout my life, although at the time I selected the topic, things were going fairly well; not great, but there were no major issues. Over the years, I've learned a lot about perseverance though and how important it is when leading from a place of integrity, honor and character.

Given Frank's education and the fact he was an avid reader, he fancied himself a skilled critic of the written word. So, he volunteered to be my editor once I'd written the piece. He wasn't at all happy when he couldn't find anything to change or correct in the finished chapter!

In his own words:

> Wooo whooo—I have met my master (or at least someone to challenge me to write better—more skillfully). I will put serious effort into reading more of your creative writing.... I'd tell you how good you are, but then your head would swell, so don't tell anyone that I said you're really, really good.

BEATEN BY A GIRL

One thing I learned quickly was not to give Frank reasons to tease me. Unfortunately, it was a lesson learned at the hands of a teenage girl.

As a martial artist, there are times during training when the students will spar each other (as in a mock fight). While we wear pads for protection and follow strict rules regarding contact, there are times when accidents happen.

One Saturday morning, I was sparring with a kid twenty-five years younger than me who is a black belt. We both happened to move in such a way that she struck me a solid blow across the jaw that sent my head snapping back. An immediate wave of dizziness and nausea had me sitting out the rest of the class.

When it was time to go home, I called Frank from the car so he could keep me company (and focused). Of course, he could tell something was a bit off, and it didn't take long for him to find out what had happened.

While he had a lot of fun teasing me about "getting beaten by a girl," he also made a long-distance assessment of my symptoms and prescribed a treatment regimen for me for once I got home. Until then, he did his best to make me smile through my pain, even if he was just being a pain himself.

Needless to say though, teasing me was one of his favorite pastimes, so it was quite a while before I lived that particular injury down!

SPIRITUAL WARFARE BEGINS

The very next day started horribly! It was a Sunday, and my main goal was to get ready to go to church. Typically, this is a relatively simple thing to accomplish. However, on this particular day, *nothing* went right.

My teenage daughter had sprained her ankle the night before and was not doing well. Yet, her commitment to her responsibilities at church made her all the more determined to go. That didn't mean she went without complaint though... With the battle still raging behind my eyes from the whiplash I'd received the day before, her whining did little to make me feel sympathetic.

When I went into my son's room to wake him up for church, he wasn't feeling well either. After a quick assessment of his condition, I decided he should stay home from church and sleep some more.

As I was helping my kids with their various ills, the poor cat tried to tell me his litter box was full and he had nowhere to go (he's an indoor cat), but I didn't respond quickly enough. He resorted to peeing on my karate uniform, which was in a pile of laundry on the floor waiting to be put into the washing machine. As I was taking care of that and cleaning his box (my daughter's responsibility), he finished his business elsewhere by pooping on the guest bed pillow.

By the time I dealt with everybody else's issues and got to my computer to send Frank a quick morning missive, I was informed by Google that I couldn't sign into my account due to "suspicious activity" and needed to verify my account again. Since that's my business email and the system my business phone number runs through, I had to take care of it right away.

Once done, I was running late for church and no longer had a moment to spare. Church itself was an emotional time that day. Three different people I held dear were each going through major, life-changing events in their lives. I felt helpless to do anything useful for them, yet my heart went out to them as they went through their respective challenges.

For one gentleman, his wife of more than sixty years was on her deathbed. We all spent time together recollecting and celebrating her life and their marriage.

Another friend was struggling with taking care of her husband who suffered from dementia. She spent some time with me sharing her recent struggles with him, and the heartbreaking decisions she was facing about their future.

Finally, there was my friend going through a terrible divorce. His wife was experiencing mental issues that drove a wedge between them because she wouldn't allow anyone to help her. In her unhappiness, she ostracized his daughter (one of the kids in my youth group) from him. Here he was, faced with a divorce he didn't want, a wife he couldn't help, and a child who believed the worst of him.

And all I could do for any of these friends was listen and pray.

When I returned home from church, Frank had left a message wondering what had happened to me since I hadn't sent my usual morning email. As I shared my morning's misadventures, his response startled me.

> I wanted to meet someone to enjoy, and while I had given up hope that ANY gurl, much less a Christ-following girl, was going to enter my life—here you MIGHT be, and we're at spiritual warfare before we've barely started. ARE YOU READY FOR ALL THIS?

It was then that he suggested we start praying together. We both believed the closer we followed God's will in our lives, the more challenges we could anticipate. So, even as early as eight days after our first phone conversation, we recognized the need to pray for strength and guidance to deal with the warfare to come (thinking, if God was happy, Satan was not)...

Ever the funny man, he concluded the conversation with the following message.

> And I'll remember to bring my own pillow if I ever stay over.... hey! I've got the trailer—I can bring my own house! Tee hee.

Digging Deeper...

At times, it can seem the closer we get to our goals, the harder the going gets, even when the goal is something we truly want and are willing to sacrifice for.

Think about the days leading up to a wedding, or the hours before the birth of your firstborn child. Chaos seems to reign. Everything is harder than it should be and then, suddenly, that thing we've been waiting for happens...

And nothing can take away the joy and sense of fulfillment we feel when everything we've hoped for comes to pass.

...Nothing that is, except that rare occasion when it's all ripped away at the last minute.

Some would rationalize that this is spiritual warfare in action. (Satan purposely trying to trip up those who are doing God's will.) Others might see it as a random set of unfortunate circumstances.

Whatever rationale or explanation you give it, there will be times when the path we walk gets rough.

There are lessons to be learned in this space.

Although it may not be easy, difficulties provide an opportunity. They are something to be grateful for. Light can only be appreciated having known the dark; warmth, the cold; joy, sadness; and contentment, want.

The rough places in our lives serve as reminders to appreciate the times when things do go "according to plan."

And it's another of those instances where knowing your purpose, knowing your goal, and being clear about the outcome you want makes all the difference in the world.

It is only then that you can look at the current difficulties and decide whether the destination is worth the discomfort of getting there.

GROWING TOGETHER

When love is new, there's a time of discovery that's precious. From the very beginning, I trusted Frank. Given the life experiences I've had, that was a minor miracle in itself, but there was something about him that made me want to remain open to him.

It became important to me *not* to put walls between us, my usual defense mechanism when someone was getting too close. I realized if I were ever going to have the healthy kind of relationship I wanted to have, I would have to be willing to be vulnerable and open to another human being, 100%. I knew, once walls went up, they were hard to tear down. I had no desire to hold back or keep Frank at arm's length. He'd won my heart, and I wanted to share everything I am with him.

Frank went through his own time of discovery as well and was equally amazed by what he was learning, sharing his life with another human being. He was in awe of the fact he was learning to read me, to recognize the different tones of my voice and what they meant, to hear the silences when they came, and to understand he'd said or done something silly or thoughtless.

He strove to be attentive, not just to what I said, but how, when and why I said it.

The more time we spent together, the more compatible it seemed we were, and I began to believe Frank was meant for me, that we had something I wanted in my life. It wasn't too long after that when he surprised me one day with a phone call.

He seemed to have a hard time figuring out which of my phone numbers did what. I told him there was really only one number he ever needed to call because it's forwarded to all of my other phone numbers. Yet, it made no sense to him.

One morning, while I was at a networking meeting for my business, my cell phone rang. Frank knew I was in a meeting but had decided to surprise me with a message for when I returned to the office. He was surprised himself when I picked up the phone and then pleased I would step out of my meeting to talk with him.

As I tried to find a quiet place in the restaurant where we could talk, I ended up standing outside the restrooms, which were down a back hall, tucked away from tables, the kitchen and the general noisiness of the place.

He commented on how surprised he was that I'd answered, and I told him it was fine; the meeting was breaking up soon anyway, and I couldn't wait to hear his voice. We joked about how hard it was when we needed to be apart (meaning not on the phone together).

Laughingly, he said, "I guess we'll just have to make this a permanent thing because I'm not willing to live without you."

Now, having been married once before and divorced, I only planned on marrying once more in my life. I wanted this next time to be my last, and I wanted everything to be "just right," including the romantically traditional, down-on-one-knee proposal. So, my joking response was "I suppose when you ask me properly, I just might say 'yes!'"

From that day onward, Frank referred to me as his wife in our conversations, and it seemed certain we were destined to marry one day. All of our thoughts and plans pointed in that direction.

A friend later told me, the next time he spoke with Frank after that, Frank started talking about going ring-shopping and how he had every intention of proposing to me properly when he finally returned to Connecticut in the fall; a trip he planned to make because I was at the end of it.

Digging Deeper…

No one likes feeling vulnerable. At least no one I know does. Do you?

To be vulnerable is defined as "capable of or susceptible to being wounded or hurt."

It seems everyone has been hurt or wounded in some way, shape or form. So, it's easy to understand why we resist being vulnerable.

But in order to protect ourselves, we put up figurative walls to shield us and keep us from harm.

The problem with that is that walls have no means of telling the difference between positive things and negative. For example, they can't discern between joy and pain.

Put up a wall, and you're equally protecting yourself from harm at the same time as distancing yourself from the people and things that bring joy and love into your life.

The answer here is another compromise. Shield yourself when necessary. Don't be vulnerable to absolutely everyone, but give people the chance to earn your trust and come "inside the walls."

The longer you stay isolated and alone within your protective walls, the easier it is to forget what it is you're missing.

Take a chance on worthy people. Allowing them unguarded access to you enables them to come to know the real you, the authentic you.

Those are the kind of friends who value you for who you are rather than what you can do. And there's no better feeling in the world than to be truly known and cared for by another.

BLENDING FAMILIES

Frank wasn't just interested in me though. He also became involved in my children's lives. He'd had a stepchild in an earlier marriage, but that had been thirty years earlier, and it had only lasted a year. When his ex-wife left, it was the last contact he had with his stepdaughter.

We talked about how he'd fit into my kids' lives. He was eager for them to like him, but had more in common with my son than my daughter.

While I hoped she would give him a chance, she took an immediate dislike to Frank. She had started seeing a boyfriend around the same time and was continually frustrated that the boy could never call because the phone line was always tied up by Frank and me. As strong-willed as her mother, it would take a lot to build a relationship there.

Yet, he did his best to support us. When my daughter, who is a dancer and an acrobat, injured her ankle in class one night, Frank walked me through everything I needed to know about getting the best medical care for her. He was pleased that his decades of experience as a first aid instructor could be put to good use.

But with my son, Frank felt more of an affinity. They had similar interests, and Frank was really looking forward to sharing new experiences with my boy.

Frank eventually asked, if we were to marry, if I would consider letting him adopt my children. He wanted us to be a family. I told him, if they wanted him to, I would love that. My kids don't have a biological father involved in their lives, and I thought it would be absolutely wonderful for them to finally have someone willing to claim them as his own.

From that point on, Frank did his best to referee arguments between my daughter and me, provide insight into issues I was having with my son, and generally stand by my side as a second parent, offering his thoughts without interfering in our relationships.

When my son decided to quit homeschooling and attend public school instead for the first time (in 6th grade), he required some additional tutoring in one subject to be at grade level when the school year started. As I was discussing this with Frank, he asked me how I was going to pay for the tutoring. I simply replied I wasn't certain at the moment, but when you're a parent, you figured something out. Sometimes it meant delaying something else or forgoing something completely, but one way or another I'd get it covered.

Frank asked if I was willing to let him help with "our son." He had every intention of being a part of our lives for a long time to come and saw no reason why his parental responsibilities shouldn't start right then. When I acknowledged that some help would be appreciated, he sent me money to cover the tutoring costs as well as to buy school supplies and clothes. It was just as much money for him to come up with as it was for me, but he wanted to do it, to show he was in this too.

When we discussed our life together (we were referring to it in the singular by then), he would wonder aloud whose children would be more problematic, my two human teenagers or his two four-legged kids. We looked forward to finding that out together!

He didn't just want to be a husband and father though, he wanted to be our provider and protector too. When we'd talk on the phone until the early morning hours, I'd invariably start to get tired. I had a schedule to keep, even if he didn't. Up at 6 am to wake the kids and get my son on the bus, then downstairs to my office to start working for the day. So, staying up late every night started to take its toll on me. But, like a high school kid, I didn't want to hang up the phone. So, we'd keep talking until one of us had to call it quits.

Frank would finish our calls reminding me that he was my centurion and would stand guard while I slept. Even though he was 1,200 miles away, I always felt safe in his keeping.

When I came across this Victor Hugo quote, I just had to share it with him. *"The supreme happiness of life is the conviction of being loved for yourself or, more correctly, being loved in spite of yourself."* I attached the following message:

> I am supremely happy! Just thought you might want to know... And YOU are the cause of it all. I blame you completely. It's all your fault.

His response was simple and to the point.

> Taking all blame.

WORKING TOGETHER

Since I own my own business, I work with a variety of clients on multiple projects each and every day. Curious about my work, Frank enjoyed hearing about the projects I was involved with. He often had relevant insights to share because of his own background and experience. So, I started running ideas by him, narrowing down options more quickly, and providing a better turn-around time than I had been on my own.

The first project we worked on together was a design project for a client's new business card. The next was the logo for the nonprofit ministry I was involved with. From there, he moved on to editing my website, reviewing my blog posts and writing projects, and being a sounding board for challenges I was working my way through.

We hoped that there would be functions within my business he could take over handling once he returned to Connecticut, and we were using this time to see whether that idea would work or not. Since he'd moved to Florida, he'd let his own computer consulting business fall into obscurity, so he had no specific employment plans when he returned. Freeing me up from my business obligations to focus on the things I did best seemed an ideal solution to both of us.

But we didn't just work together in my business. We worked together finding solutions to everyday problems too, like the time I ran into technical difficulties paying my mortgage online. It was the weekend, and the grace period was ending. If I didn't pay it then somehow, I'd be hit with a late fee I didn't want to have to pay because of issues with their website. Sharing my frustration and difficulties with Frank, he suggested I pay by phone instead, since the pay-by-phone fee was significantly less than the late fee.

While it was a simple answer, I was so fixated on how I had intended to pay that my mind wasn't open enough to see another solution until it was pointed out to me. We did that for each other regularly, and we both loved it. As Frank put it, we didn't just find a solution together, we found a better solution. That's how we anticipated our life together to be.

As a result, we found ourselves using the term "longing" frequently in our messages to one another. I summarized it this way in one email conversation.

> "Longing" is a good word for now. There's a part of me that wants to take our time and savor these incredible feelings and experiences that I truly didn't think were going to happen again. And another part of me that simply wants to know how it's all going to turn out. Sometimes, there are reasons to envy God. He's enjoying this time with us while we experience these new things, at the same time as already knowing how it's all going to work out.

The future seemed to hold so much promise, but only time would tell what God's plans were for us.

Digging Deeper...

Everyone likes to believe they're capable of "thinking outside of the box." Don't they?

And yet, it's easy when we're living our lives unchallenged to become complacent. We do the things we want to, the way we want to, and resist change when it's suggested.

However, there is a wise saying that goes "two are better than one" (Ecclesiastes 4:9a).

When there are two (or more), it requires us to communicate, share the best of ourselves, and compromise. This enables us to come up with a better solution than we may be capable of on our own, or at least more well-thought-out decisions.

The complacency that comes from living life unchallenged keeps us from growing, from improving, from learning, and from thriving.

We get locked into doing the things we've always done the way we've always done them and passing that on to future generations to do the same way.

Complacency is the enemy of innovation. It kills the urge to create. It takes pleasure in the norm.

One of the most refreshing things in life is to surround yourself with people who challenge you to be more, do more, and think more than you ever would on your own.

As your comfort zone stretches and expands, you grow into a more capable version of yourself, which brings you one step closer to living a gratifying life.

DUELING POEMS

Sometimes, new love inspires us to try our hand at things we haven't done in a long time. For Frank, it inspired him to write me a few poems. The first was a silly verse, hurriedly thrown together and inserted in the body of an email along with some other thoughts; nothing worthy of note.

A week or so later, he made his first real attempt at writing a poem for me, and it left me speechless.

> I could easily say I love you,
> Just as easily as *je t'adore*.
> I step back not for hurting,
> But to guard the open door.
>
> Your heart is precious to me,
> And your body and your mind;
> Our faiths' importance paramount
> As our lives become entwined.
>
> So arise my love, my fair one
> And come away with me
> For all the time God offers
> We'll be what we can be.

He wasn't as impressed by my poem for him (because it didn't rhyme and he believed it had to), but I found myself reading this one over and over again. Here was someone pouring his heart out to me, whose hopes and desires were aligned with mine, who was willing to put my needs ahead of his, and our Lord's will above both of ours. In this simple poem, I saw the framework for a Christ-centered marriage laid out, and I prayed God would offer us a full and wonderful life together.

There were times though when Frank would wonder at the miracle of God bringing us together at all, at the same time as sensing it wasn't going to last nearly as long as either of us wanted. One time, he wondered if we could lobby God in case our being together wasn't part of His plan, or if we could just sneak off unnoticed. "After all," he said, "God let the Israelites wander for forty years, perhaps He'd let us too."

The first time he told me he was afraid we wouldn't have long enough together, I tried to push aside his concerns. I assumed he was referring to our age difference or the fact that, in both of us being alone so long, we might find it difficult to compromise.

Sometimes now I wonder if he really knew our time together was destined to be short-lived.

When we sought God's will in our relationship, it was hard to figure out sometimes what was our own desire and what was from Him. I put it this way once:

> We have to wonder, with such depth of feeling (not just lust or infatuation, but genuine feeling), perhaps God has granted us both the desires of our hearts already. And it's not a matter of waiting for Him to reveal His plan, but for us to be able to trust that this is of Him. We still need His guidance and leading hand, but it's a different way of viewing the situation. Perhaps we need to pray that He opens our eyes. His will may already be revealed, and we're just not "getting it." What do you think?

Dueling Poems

The struggle to understand God at work is as old as the day is long. Brief moments of clarity may come, but the rest of the time, it's often obscured by the busyness in our hearts and minds.

THE GIFT OF DIRT

One of Frank's favorite pastimes was serving as the moderator to the local chapter of the ReUseIt group we met through. This group allowed local folks to post items they no longer wanted, but that were in gently used condition, so others who did want them could claim them. It also allowed people who were looking for a specific item to post what it was they were looking for. Ultimately, it saved people money and saved perfectly usable items from hitting the landfills.

As moderator, Frank got to see all of the offers being made before they were sent out to the group. One day, he was approving posts while we were on the phone together. He suddenly chuckled and asked if I needed any dirt. The funny thing was, I did! So, he connected me with the group member who was offering it. I spent the next few weeks picking up a few yards' worth of dirt in the back of my SUV every day or two, hoping to fill a sinkhole in my front yard.

Frank had all sorts of fun with that. He loved the idea that he'd been the "provider" of the dirt and, since he was still down in Florida, he didn't have to actually move any of it.

He often was on the phone with me while I was shoveling, loading, unloading and tamping the dirt, and marveled at my stamina. Having him on the other end of the line, keeping me company as I worked wearing a headset, was always an incredible blessing. It felt like he was right there, and I had fun teasing him about his laziness and asking when he was going to pick up a shovel and help me out.

It's not often that a man can give a woman a gift of dirt and she's happy about it, but such was the nature of our unusual relationship!

PRAYING ON OUR KNEES

Early in our relationship, Frank and I established a habit of prayer. When we prayed together each night at bedtime, our minds were quieted and focused on Jesus first, the tremendous blessing we'd been given in each other second, and those we loved third.

He often prayed for my concerns and needs, lifting up my friends in Tanzania, where I've done missionary work, praying for Willie, the gentleman in my church who had recently lost his wife of sixty-six years to cancer, and praying for the four babies in my circle of friends who were all born within a week of one another, including his favorite, "little Dean," who almost didn't make it.

One time, we prayed together for a friend who had been a vendor at a local fair. During the day, someone stole his cash box. While the money was important, most of it was in receipt form (credit card charges to be processed later in the day). Even more important was a flash drive that contained the manuscript for the book he was working on. Frank and I earnestly prayed for the return of the cash box with all its valuables intact. We both cheered when we learned that the box had been found two blocks away and had been turned in to the police. While $20 worth of loose change was missing, all of the receipts and the flash drive were still in the box. Frank's response? "Yeah, God!"

When we prayed together, Frank always asked for God's blessing upon me, my children, and my business, and wasn't afraid to be humorous with God. He figured that if God gave him such wit, He must take delight in it. So, there were no rote or somber prayers from Frank. He brought his whole being into his prayers, sometimes laughing and teasing God and me, and every once in a while, crying. I'm so very blessed to have witnessed that.

Frank rarely prayed for himself but had shared enough of his concerns and challenges that I was able to pray for him as he had for me.

His major concern was his relationship with his father. Frank went down to Florida from his home in Connecticut when his father had fallen and broken his leg. Frank had hoped that by being there for him and helping him recover, he would somehow finally get the recognition and approval from his father that he'd been craving all his life.

Unfortunately, that didn't happen. His father wasn't a hard man, but the two of them continually disappointed each other, and neither was willing to look beyond their dashed expectations to see into the heart of the other. Motives were assumed and assigned, and there was little room for open communication as a result.

All I could do at that point was pray. So, every night, I prayed for healing and reconciliation between these two men. I prayed that they have ears to hear one another and eyes to see and hearts open enough to listen to each other. Then I patiently waited to see what God would do.

It was an incredible blessing to be able to pray for my loved one. My mother had prayed over me before, as had a pastor. But there is nothing more intimate than a couple that prays together and for each other. I can assure you of that and am so thankful to have had the experience...

Our prayer time often lasted an hour or longer, always on our knees, and covered many topics. But they always began and ended with gratitude to have found one another.

Praying on my knees was a new experience for me. My relationship with Jesus Christ is an ongoing personal relationship. Prayer takes the form of frequent conversations with no prescribed expectations or rote methods required. I pray when I'm driving. I pray when I'm singing. I pray when I'm in the shower, washing dishes, or teaching my children. My prayers may be flashed heavenward in a few seconds, or I may spend a prolonged period of time talking with my Lord, just as any other relationship I have.

Yet, the first time Frank and I went to pray together, I was getting ready to settle comfortably into a chair when Frank said "God's telling me to kneel." The power of that statement was vast.

Here was a man with neuropathy in his hands and feet, who found it hard to be physically active. Yet, he chose to kneel while we prayed because he desired that our relationship always be God-honoring. That first night, Frank heeded God's prompting and knelt, and I followed suit. If he could kneel in his physically diminished capacity, then so could I with my younger, martial arts-trained body.

Little did we know that night when we chose to kneel that we'd be in conversation with God for over an hour, or that all of our future prayer times together would be spent on our knees for lengthy periods of time. Yet, it became our habit of prayer together, kneeling before God and worshipping Him.

I often prayed for patience, asking God to reveal His will for us and to help me to be patient while we waited on His timing. Every time I made that request, Frank would chastise me. He'd remind me that the only way to learn patience was to practice it, and I was effectively asking God to create situations where I'd have to be patient. He teased that God would probably keep him down in Florida another year, just to help me learn patience. Little did he know he'd never leave there...

It was hard to come up with another term besides "patience," though, that conveyed a similar enough meaning. The whole point was I wanted us to both be clear that we were following God's leading and not our own.

A friend has since suggested that the better thing to pray for is mental discipline and spiritual strength. I think perhaps he was right, although I alternate between prayers for those and prayers for peace and direction while living within God's will for my life.

Digging Deeper...

For some people, patience is a four-letter word. It stands in the way between them and what they want. They think many steps ahead of where they currently are, with their eyes solely on the goal.

Can you think of a time when all that you wanted was just out of reach? Remember that feeling of being so intent on obtaining the prize? Nothing else mattered. Your focus was complete. The goal was so near you could taste it.

There are times in life when that's a very good thing. It allows you to block out the distractions along the way to accomplishing your purpose.

While knowing where you're headed and what you want to accomplish is important and something I advise if you want to live an intentional life, don't stay so focused on the outcome that you miss your surroundings.

Impatience deprives us of the pleasure of being right where we're currently at and enjoying the journey of becoming who and what we were meant to be.

The only thing we have is the here and now. Patience is the gift that allows us to enjoy the present.

STUDYING THE WORD

Soon after we started praying together each night, we had a theological discussion one evening. Frank wanted to understand more about spiritual gifts. As we talked about them a bit, he asked where he could find that passage in the Bible. I pointed him to 1 Corinthians 12:7-11.

He'd been raised to read the King James Version (KJV) of the Bible, but I had other translations I preferred. So, after reading his KJV and still wanting to understand more clearly, I read the same passage from the NIV (New International Version, 1984 ed.) and then from the NLT (New Living Translation).

We discussed these gifts because he'd been told at a young age that he had the gift of discernment, and he'd always wanted to understand whether that was truly a gift of the spirit as outlined in the New Testament, or simply an interpretation of the minister who'd named his gift. This discussion led to looking at the fruit of the Spirit as well in Galatians 5:22-23.

As we spoke, Frank confessed it had been years (decades perhaps) since he'd last read his Bible, even though he'd once studied to be a minister. Over the years, I've spent many hours in study and reflection on the Bible, and so my familiarity with it was greater than his own.

Thankfully, he decided we should add Bible study to our nightly routine, prior to prayer time. Since I wasn't interested in struggling through the King James Version, and he didn't want to read the NIV, we settled on using my favorite translation, the NLT. Since he didn't have a copy of that handy, we agreed to use a website as the basis of our reading and study.

Each night, as the day was wrapping up, we'd get on the phone with our computers before us and take turns reading a chapter aloud to each other, then discussing it. We intended to read two chapters a night but often enjoyed the reading and discussion so much that we read four or more.

We started our daily reading in Galatians since that's where we were at the time we agreed on the routine and continued reading through Colossians. Then, we went back to Acts and started our readings there.

It was so much fun to study together. Frank, with his ever-present wit, would read using various voices or throwing things in there just to see if I was paying attention. Subtle alterations like "gals" instead of "women," "sad sissies" instead of "Sadducees," and "cowboys" instead of "soldiers" were all there just to keep me on my toes. Some may have considered it sacrilegious. All I knew was, I had to pay attention and read along or he'd have me lost in no time! Bible study had never been this much fun before.

As time drew on, Frank confessed to me that he'd never felt as close to God as he did at this time in his life. Knowing this was a great comfort to me.

THE TEST OF A RELATIONSHIP

After having been alone for so long, I wasn't willing to settle for just any relationship. I believed I was ready to be in a healthy relationship, and I needed someone capable of that too.

Since I'd been raised in a dysfunctional home, I didn't have much experience with what a healthy relationship would look like. However, two things were key to me.

One was that I wanted a relationship where there were no walls between us. I'd become a master over the years at building walls to protect myself and knew how hard they were to take down once they were erected. I decided to trust Frank and his intentions toward me. Therefore, to have the kind of relationship I wanted, I prohibited myself from building any walls. There were no questions he could ask that I wasn't willing to answer, no matter how difficult or uncertain I was about the response.

That even included an early discussion of my views regarding sex in our relationship. My earlier relationships were often complicated (at best) when sex was introduced into the relationship too soon. I have a healthy appreciation of physical intimacy and was looking forward to the possibility of it in my life again. But I wanted our first time together to be on our wedding night. This wasn't because of any sanctimonious condemnation of sex outside of marriage, but because I wanted to honor God with our relationship and our bodies. I didn't want our coupling to be simply a physical act, but an act of worship for the God who made us for each other.

So, Frank and I talked openly about what the Bible had to say about sexual relationships. Initially, Frank felt that the admonition not to have sex outside of marriage only applied to virgins or to people who had never been married before. Since we'd both been married and divorced, he wasn't too certain that the biblical tenet of saving sex for marriage applied to us. Yet, when we came to Ephesians 5 in our reading together, our prayers for insight were fully answered there, as Paul spoke so openly about God's will and plan for relationships. After that, even if I'd wanted to change my mind about waiting (and there were times when I did), there's no way Frank would have agreed.

The other thing that was key to me was that we needed to be able to communicate freely. Not having walls was a part of that. More importantly, we needed to feel comfortable sharing our thoughts and ideas, free from reproach, correction or condemnation. That was easy enough to do most of the time. We had similar worldviews and values, although a distinctly different sense of humor. However, Frank made every effort to be considerate of my sensibilities and to refrain from the off-color or offensive jokes he so easily shared early on in our relationship.

About a month after we started seeing each other, he said something that really hurt my feelings or angered me. (I can't recall which now.) It's been so long, I don't even remember the specific situation.

Instead, what stuck in my memory was the realization that we'd come to the first test of our relationship. I had to tell him how he'd affected me. My past experience made me feel ill at the thought of confronting him. In my mind, the only possible conclusion was a fight, and I really didn't want to fight with him. I was afraid I might lose him if I did.

In some ways, that argument was probably the best thing for us. It gave me a chance to put into practice what I believed was the right response in a healthy relationship. Despite my heart trying to beat its way out of my chest as my stomach fought to claw its way up my throat, I was able to slide the words out of my mouth to tell him how his actions made me feel.

As I tensed for his response, anticipating an argument, he surprised me by validating my feelings instead. He acknowledged what he'd done, apologized for unintentionally hurting me, and thanked me for being vulnerable enough with him to open up to him. To be affirmed in that way was huge for me.

I was incredibly blessed by his response and his loving care for my feelings in the process.

Digging Deeper...

Are you afraid of confrontation?

For some of us, the very idea of sharing our thoughts and our desires leaves us feeling paralyzed. What will the consequences be? Will I pay too high a price for having an opinion?

At the heart of the matter, fear of confrontation is a trust issue. At some point in our lives, when it mattered most to us, we weren't allowed the opportunity to share what we needed, or we were ridiculed for what we wanted.

Perhaps a boss disregarded our project input, a teacher told us our questions were stupid, our first crush laughed at us when they found out how we felt, or a parent treated us as a child much longer than they should have.

Whatever the reason, we've come to believe that standing up for ourselves or inserting our thoughts into a conversation is a bad idea. It will only bring pain, shame or embarrassment.

We trusted someone to value what we had to offer, and that trust was broken. It doesn't matter if the response we got was ridicule, anger, embarrassment or haranguing. We expected tolerance, acceptance and support, and didn't get it.

But not everyone deserves that lack of trust and not every confrontation has to turn out that way. In a healthy relationship (whether personal or professional), it's important to build the kind of connection that allows both parties the opportunity to express their thoughts and ideas without censure.

Remember when you were little being told "if you want a friend, learn how to be a friend?" I say, if you want someone you can trust, practice the art of truly listening and being trustworthy with what you hear.

TOO MUCH QUIET

During the last week of August, Frank started feeling poorly. He had a few days of nausea and diarrhea that left him weak and exhausted. While I'd thought his bouts with insomnia and his diabetic neuropathy were a lot to deal with, this took everything to a whole new level.

Whereas before, Frank would sleep for hours during the day (and be awake all night), now he slept for days on end. Before this illness, we'd been spending twelve to fourteen hours a day on the phone with each other, keeping each other company as we went about our days. Now, I went days without hearing from him.

Since it was leading into the Labor Day weekend, I was concerned about whether he needed help and if I'd be able to reach anyone over the holiday. Each time we had spoken, I'd asked him to go see a doctor. But, because he was uninsured, he didn't want to incur the expense. He was saving his money for the trip home to be with me…

After a few more days of not hearing from him, and at a loss for what to do, I called the nursing home where his father was residing. I asked an attendant there if it was possible to send his father's right-hand man, Palmer, over to check in on him.

Boy! Did that get me in a world of trouble with Frank afterward! He resented Palmer's relationship with his father, feeling that he'd stepped into shoes Frank was supposed to fill.

When we talked about it later, he told me I had overreacted. He accused me of having sent a horde of people to his house. As he related the events, they came in, disturbed his rest, gave him some kind of drug (or so he believed in his addled state), wound up the dogs, who wouldn't shut up, and they wouldn't leave when he told them to.

I have no idea who actually checked on him, or how (or why) they decided he was alright to leave alone. I never received a report back from *anyone* saying they had gone to see him. And if they had, I find it hard to believe they would have decided he was well enough to leave alone. But, apparently, they did.

Prior to falling ill, Frank had been making plans to come north to see me. At this point, I began talking about making a trip south to check on him and help him get back on his feet. It was hard to accept, but he asked me not to. He didn't want our first meeting to be that way. He had dreamed of what our first date would be like and flying 1,200 miles to come nurse him when he was ill was not at all aligned with the romantic date he had planned for us.

Unfortunately, he continued to worsen instead of improving. This period marked the beginning of odd visions, terrifying dreams, and a deep and clinging sleep that left him disoriented, frightened and weak. Rarely leaving his bed, he stopped eating and drinking, for the most part, only making it out to the kitchen every few days.

He began to believe someone was there in the house with him. He'd tell me about a shadowy figure that sat in the chair in the corner of his room while he was in bed. Every time he'd look at the chair, it would be empty. Yet, out of the corner of his eye, he'd sometimes see someone there simply waiting. He didn't know whether or not to be scared and simply found it frustrating that he couldn't figure out what was going on.

Once again, I urged him to call the doctor. He needed medical attention. He'd been sick for three weeks at this point, with no signs of improvement and worsening symptoms. When he refused, I wrote down absolutely everything I could think of about his health and sent it to a friend of mine who is an ICU nurse. I asked her if she had any advice for me. She reviewed the information and told me I needed to do whatever I could to get him medical attention. His blood sugars were dangerously high, and other things in my report indicated the presence of inflammation or an infection. Given his medical history, he needed to seek treatment as soon as possible.

By this time though, his demeanor had changed as well. Everything became an argument. So, try as I would, he refused to go to the doctor or the hospital. He knew by this time they'd admit him to work on him and that was only going to cost all that much more money; money he didn't have and didn't want to ask his father for.

So, he convinced himself I was wrong and accused me of being inconsiderate because I wouldn't just let him sleep. He insisted I was tormenting him by calling all the time, even though I was only calling every few days at that point.

His mood would swing from loving to intolerable and back again in a matter of minutes, and I found it harder and harder to bear, especially in light of the idyllic time we'd shared earlier.

He never felt well enough to read the Bible or pray together anymore, always promising we'd try the next night or in the morning. But it didn't happen.

When Frank became ill, everything changed. His temper shortened. He became frustrated, irritable and frequently unpleasant. My trusting heart was repeatedly trodden upon, which I excused knowing that he wasn't feeling well, believing it would only be short-term, that he'd be well again soon and our life would resume our normal routine.

By early October, he wasn't any better. I seriously considered breaking up with him. Yet, I didn't want to be "that woman" who abandons her significant other just because he's ill. So, I held out hope that he'd begin to recover soon and all would be well again, even as I wrestled with feelings that evoked too many memories of the verbal and emotional abuse I'd suffered as a child.

Two weeks later, I began to think my prayers were being answered. The hostility subsided. Frank's humor, so long absent, began to peek through again. He was weak. He was tired. He'd lost a lot of weight. But he was staying awake for longer periods and, most importantly to me at the time, he started to joke with me again. He even set a date to start reading the Bible and praying together again.

It seemed we had turned a corner.

HOPE ARISES
AND THEN SWAN DIVES

As his sense of humor returned and he started eating and drinking again, he recognized that most of his neuropathy seemed to have quieted down. His hands and feet didn't cause him much pain at all, which he was thrilled about especially since he hadn't taken any of his medications in weeks.

Over the next few days, we talked but only in brief conversations once or twice a day. Our last call lasted less than two minutes.

He was upright and semi-mobile, but he was having palpitations. He had a prescription medication for that, but in the extended weeks of his illness, he had no idea where his pills had ended up. He was certain if he just sat for a bit, he'd be fine.

While he was happy to talk with me, he wanted to rest and promised to call me when he woke up. At 6:15 pm on Wednesday, October 19, 2011, I hung up the phone, determined to wait for his call.

Thursday came and went with no call from him. Halfway through Friday, I promised myself that if he didn't call by Saturday, I'd call him. I wholeheartedly believed he'd call on Friday and I wouldn't have to worry about it.

But then Saturday came and there was still no word. I called, just once, and left a message. Then again on Sunday, and on Monday, and on Tuesday. I wanted to call to have someone check on him again, but recalled how upset he'd been the last time I did that. So, I didn't.

Wednesday came and went and still no answer. I needed to do *something*. So, on Thursday, I reached out to Frank's best friend, Jeff, to see if he'd heard from him any more recently than I had. But it had been a few weeks since they last talked.

Jeff had told Frank what an idiot he was being for not getting checked out by a doctor. Frank thanked him for his opinion and told him to go take a flying leap. That was the last time either of them spoke to each other.

Since Jeff was here in Connecticut as well, the only thing he could recommend was that I call the sheriff in Red Leaf, the town where Frank lived, and ask that they do a wellness check.

I held out hope that somehow it wouldn't be necessary. I found it hard to gather my courage enough to risk upsetting Frank again. So, I waited some more.

When the next morning dawned, I realized I couldn't wait any longer…

FINDING THE COURAGE TO CALL

Following Jeff's advice, I finally got up the courage to call the Red Leaf sheriff's office. While I'd looked up the number on the internet many times in recent weeks, I'd closed the browser every time without picking up the phone.

Recognizing that the weekend was soon to start and I might have to go a few more days with no further information, I called the sheriff's office at 1 pm. I explained the situation. My boyfriend lived there in town, while I was in Connecticut so couldn't check on him myself. We typically spoke many times a day for many hours a day. He'd been sick recently, and I hadn't heard from him in over a week. My messages and calls had gone unanswered, and I was concerned for his welfare. I also explained that when I called his cell phone, it went straight to voicemail, which meant the battery had most likely died and Frank wouldn't be able to call for help himself if he needed it.

Per Jeff's instruction, I asked them to do a "wellness check." The dispatcher took Frank's name and address, and my contact information, and told me they'd get back to me when they knew something more.

I continued to work, trying to occupy my mind with things that needed to be done for my clients. Yet, as the afternoon drew to a close, I started to become concerned that perhaps I wasn't going to hear from them. I decided I would follow up at 4:40 if they hadn't called before, assuming everyone would get off work for the weekend around 5.

At 4 pm though, the phone rang... The date was October 28, 2011, and my world was about to shatter...

THE AWFUL NEWS

The man on the other end of the phone line identified himself as a deputy from the Red Leaf sheriff's office. He asked for me by name and then asked for my address.

As he spoke his next words, I knew my worst fears were being realized. "Normally, we send someone out with this kind of news, but I have no way of sending someone to you." All I could think was *That's a line straight out of a TV show*, thankful there wasn't going to be that dreaded knock at my door, but not wanting him to go on; my heart screaming at him *Stop talking! Just stop!*

But he didn't hear me...

He then informed me there was indeed someone deceased at the address I'd provided and, based on his condition, he had been for some time.

I couldn't even acknowledge his words... I knew that if Frank were gone, there was nothing I could do about it, and I couldn't face the possibility it was true.

I latched on to the dogs. "And the dogs? Are they okay? It's been nine days since I last spoke to Frank!"

He informed me that the dogs were part of the reason for the delay in calling me back. As they approached Frank's home, the dogs started barking. They had to wait for Animal Control to arrive on the scene and remove the animals before they could enter the house.

One of the dogs was in very bad shape and had to be carried out. He thought something had happened to the dog during the past week because he wasn't able to walk right. I told him immediately that it had to be Bear and shared with him what I knew of the physical handicap Bear was born with.

Both dogs were being taken to the local animal shelter where the shelter officials would decide whether they could be saved and what to do with them.

Urgently, I informed the deputy that I wanted them. I had no idea how to make that happen, but they were *not* to be put down. He promised to make sure Animal Control knew that.

From there, questions returned to Frank, and we both answered each other's inquiries to the best of our abilities.

I told him how and where to find Frank's father, even though we'd never met. I replayed the last few weeks of our contact, letting him know that our last brief conversation had ended at 6:15 pm on October 19.

He made notes and informed me that the coroner had just arrived to pick up the body. He made it clear that whoever was in the house had been dead for some time in the Florida heat with no air conditioning and the windows still closed. He believed it was likely I was the last person to speak to Frank, but that if he found anything else out, he'd let me know.

In the meantime, he told me the body would be taken to the Jacksonville Medical Examiner's office. I was going to have to follow up with them on Monday as to the next steps there.

I took down his name and contact information, as well as that of the medical examiner, and we ended our conversation.

I desperately wanted to fall apart, but my son was upstairs and my daughter needed to be picked up from her performing arts school soon. I knew I needed to see to their needs first.

I made one last phone call, this time to my mother. In a few brief words, I told her that Frank was dead. I know she asked questions. She had plans that evening, but did I want her to come over instead? Was I okay? I told her not to change her plans, but no, I wasn't alright. I did ask her to bring my daughter home because I knew I couldn't—shouldn't—drive.

After a few more minutes of talking, she told me she would pick up my daughter, and then she was coming over. In the meantime, she called my pastor to ask him to check on me. Something in my tone of voice left her frightened and concerned. She knew I was on the edge and, with all that I'd been through in my life, she'd never heard that in me before.

It was only when I hung up the phone again that I finally fell apart.

Digging Deeper...

That moment when your world came crashing down... Do you remember it?

Time slowed. You saw it coming but were helpless to prevent it from happening.

I invite you to spend a minute thinking about it. Really look at it. Take it back out from where you've buried it deep. Remember the experience.

What was happening around you? Did you "put on a brave face" or did you collapse under the weight of the world settling on your shoulders?

Are there little details you latched onto that seem silly or inappropriate in hindsight?

Are there things you wish you'd said or done that you didn't? Or things you did say or do that you wish you hadn't?

Who was the first person you called to share the news with? How did they react?

In one second, your life changed irrevocably. Today, it doesn't even matter whether it was your fault or not. Your life is marked with the consequences of the event, never to be the same again...

Have you been anchored in the past by this event? It doesn't have to leave you there.

There is no right or wrong way to grieve, no matter what the loss. Your heart was broken. Your life changed forever.

Grant yourself permission to feel the pain. Anyone who has ever suffered the loss of a dream will know that you need to.

And when you're ready, let's move on together.

A STORM WITHIN AND A STORM WITHOUT

Try as I might, I don't remember the rest of that night. I do know that my pastor came and spent some time with me, but I have no idea how long it was.

I know my mother picked up my daughter and brought her home, then stayed with me for a time, but I don't recall what we said to one another.

We've never had the kind of relationship where I've sought to be comforted by her. Typically, I'm the comforter. But I do remember melting into her arms, crumpled on the floor, and just sobbing, uncertain what I was even crying for or what would ever comfort me again.

At some point, I tried to pull myself together long enough to make an appearance to my children. As a single parent, I've never had the luxury of "just losing it." Yet, I knew this time was going to be a struggle.

I did my best to be reassuring, but matter-of-fact. Frank was gone. My heart hurt more than it had ever hurt before in my life. That's all I knew.

I went to my bedroom, shut the door, pulled the covers over my head, and tried to sleep. I was mentally, physically and emotionally flattened. Tears ripped me apart, and the force of my cries scared even me.

Eventually, my mother took my daughter to a friend's house and took my son home with her. The greatest comfort she could offer me at that point was to grant me the time and space I needed to grieve.

I awoke the next day to an empty house and what seemed to me an empty life. However, the storms had only just begun.

By 4 o'clock that afternoon, it had already been snowing for a couple of hours. Then, the power went out. The storm that was raging inside of me as I railed against God, life and Frank was soon reflected in the conditions outside. Not only did the snow start to pile up quickly, but the trees were still heavily laden with leaves. Branches, as well as whole trees, started to topple.

One tree in my backyard broke in two different directions. A large branch fell westward, landing on top of the chain-link fence in the backyard, the future playground to two orphaned dogs. The other half of the tree fell eastward, landing on another section of the fence after sliding off the house. The snow was still steadily falling, and it was impossible to go outside and assess the damage. All I could do was wait for the storm to pass, and then take stock of things at that time.

Ultimately, my kids stayed with friends and my mother for most of the next week. Our house went five days without power or telephone. That meant no outside contact, no heat, no water, no internet, and no physical comfort.

Given my inconsolable state, that seemed only fitting. While my children stayed elsewhere and were kept warm, happy and dry, I waged battle against the elements and God, alternately pleading with and challenging Him to take me too; clearing snow, cutting felled trees, hurling the cut wood as far and as hard as I could. I stayed outside in the wind and snow, not caring or realizing how cold I felt on the outside because everything felt busted on the inside.

While rage had been a frequent friend of mine in my younger days, it had been years since I had experienced the overwhelming lack of control that accompanies it. I spent those early days alternating between the mindless rampages of a wild beast and the spent whimperings of an overwrought child.

When neighbors came to see if I needed anything, I found it difficult to even label who Frank was in relation to me. While he had jokingly proposed, I'd jokingly deferred until he asked me properly. Yet, from that time on, we began making wedding plans, talking about where we wanted to honeymoon and live, and sharing dreams of what our future would be like. So, he wasn't just my boyfriend either.

In prayer, he had begun referring to me as his wife and before God we both believed that was so. We each believed we were intended for the other. Yet, in this world's eyes, we lacked a piece of paper. I soon defaulted to referring to him as my fiancé. It was easiest that way. We were promised to each other, even if I hadn't actually said "yes" when he asked me and didn't possess a ring yet.

Nothing was easy anymore. Each night, I slept in my own bed, despite the freezing temperatures. After so many nights spent talking with Frank on the phone before drifting off to sleep in the wee hours of the morning, I couldn't imagine there being any comfort anywhere else in the world. Staying in my own bed, replaying his voice in my head as he promised to stand guard while I slept... It was the only solace I could find.

Digging Deeper...

Rage. Fear. Despair. That overwhelming sense that life will never be the same and there's not a thing you can do about it. Hopelessness settles in. Defeat.

After a devastating event, it seems impossible to have long, in-depth conversations about anything. Simple decisions are impossible to make. Questions you've been answering all of your life suddenly have no meaning.

Are you tired? Are you hungry? Do you want us to come? Do you want us to leave? I don't know... I don't know. I don't know!

The anger builds.

I remember times when it seemed the only thing I could do was remind myself to breathe. I'd squeeze my eyes shut tight, curl into a ball willing the world to go away, and just take the next breath. I couldn't commit to anything more than that.

It was like being on a roller coaster and thinking "if I can just get over the next few minutes, this feeling will go away."

And don't talk to me about God. Don't tell me you're praying for me. God doesn't care. God's betrayed me. God did this!

In the days following Frank's death, I hated God.

Perhaps you can relate...

Yet, you know what I found out? He could take it. He understood, and he loved me anyway.

He didn't interject himself into my grief, but he surrounded me with people who cared. He was like the wind in the trees. I couldn't see him, but I could see and feel the impact he was having.

He wept with me. He cried to see his child in such pain. And he weeps with you as well.

Whether you believe in God or not, know that your anger is natural. Your grief is expected. And you are still loved.

IN THE AFTERMATH OF ALFRED

Those five and a half days without power after Storm Alfred were disorienting ones to me. I often thought it ironic that it was named "Alfred," when it could have so easily been named "Albert," Frank's given name.

Each day was spent getting up, feeling disoriented, knowing the world had dramatically shifted, and still trying to orient myself on what it all meant. Without the kids at home, I didn't have to worry about getting them up or feeding them. Most mornings saw me getting out of bed and going outside to gather a bucket of snow to dump in the bathtub, hoping it would stay warm enough in the house for it to melt to use for toilet water later in the day.

I'd find some way to get myself together for the day and gather up my laptop, computer cable, cell phone, clean clothes and toiletries, so I could go to my mother's house, get cleaned up, and then either spend some time there or, more likely, hang out at Starbucks for the day so I could use my computer. I spent the time researching, making notes, trying to figure out how to get Frank's affairs in order, and pretending to do some work, at the same time as placing calls that needed to be made.

The first call I made Monday morning was to the Jacksonville Medical Examiner's office, as soon as they opened. They took my information to ensure I had the right to speak to them. They saw my name on the police report. For whatever reason, even though I wasn't family, they were willing to talk to me and answer my questions.

They told me they hadn't begun processing the body yet and probably would not get to it until later that day. They couldn't tell me how long it would take once they started. Unfortunately, in the time after his death, his body had decayed so much, they needed to make an identification using his fingerprints or dental records, and they currently didn't have anything to compare those to. Since he had no identification on him at the time of his death, this was their only option. As far as they were concerned, we were assuming it was Frank, but only because this body was found in Frank's house.

I was told to call back in another day or two, once they'd had time to begin processing the body and try to figure things out. It was hard waiting. Sometimes wildly hopeful thoughts crept in. Perhaps it wasn't Frank! But if it weren't, what was a body doing in his house? That train of thought held its own peril for my bruised psyche.

There are times when we wait in life that have such different impacts on us. I remember the many hours spent waiting for the birth of my firstborn child and the anticipation of the joy that was to come. There's no joy in waiting to speak to a medical examiner about the identification of a loved one, and yet there's something just as compelling; needing that event to take place because life can't move forward until it does.

His body would not be released without a positive identification, so no funeral arrangements could be made, no obituary posted, no closure could be had until his body was identified.

I had waited until Monday morning too to reach out for the first time to Frank's father. I knew he was elderly and in a nursing home, but I didn't know whether or not he even knew I existed.

When I'd spoken to the sheriff's deputy the day Frank's body was discovered, I had asked that my contact information be passed to Frank's father, so that if he wanted to speak to me, he could. Since I hadn't heard from him, I didn't know if it was because of the storm's impact or because he hadn't even tried. So, picking up the phone to call him on Monday was a hard thing to do. My heart was pounding in my chest.

Digging Deeper...

Are you a "fixer?"

Oftentimes, when we go through difficult circumstances, we throw ourselves into activity (work) in order to avoid the pain and discomfort we're going through.

To feel the full impact of everything that's happening would just be too overwhelming. So, we find other things to distract ourselves with. We take care of others, deferring our own needs. We start trying to fill in the gap that's been left in our lives. Or we seek someone to blame.

Our lives become filled with the mundane so we can avoid the extraordinary pain threatening to engulf us if we let it.

Having a To-Do list saves us from reflecting on what's going on. We may justify it by saying it's what's expected of us.

The problem is, when we avoid what needs to be dealt with, we stuff the feelings. I can assure you, they're not going to go away on their own.

Left unattended, pain takes root in our lives, festering and causing even greater pain.

It's important to be sensitive to the needs of others who are also affected by the changed circumstances in our lives. I'm not saying to ignore their needs. I am saying though, you need to see to your own needs as well.

When I was a new single parent, a dear friend of mine would gently remind me that I needed to take care of myself if I wanted to be able to give my child the best of what I had to give. Taking care of your own needs at this time is not selfishness. It's survival.

CALLING PAPA FRANK

It was hard when I was finally able to call the nursing home and speak to Frank's Dad, because I didn't know what kind of reception to expect, and I didn't know for certain whether he even knew of my existence.

Added to that, I soon discovered that, in identifying myself to the nursing home staff as Frank's girlfriend when I called, I'd caused some confusion. They were perplexed at first. They had always known *my* Frank as "Frankie," something my Frank had never admitted to (and most likely hated—he'd told me once about a boss who insisted on calling him by his given name and his response that made it clear the only name he'd ever answer to was "Frank").

His father was known to the nursing home staff as "Frank." Both of these men went by their middle name in lieu of their given names, which they only used as initials. To distinguish between the two, instead of using their given names, they were Frank and Frankie.

I found it impossible at first to call my Frank "Frankie," such a diminutive name for someone who had become such a huge part of my life. So, a friend of Frank's and I started referring to them as "Frank" and "Papa Frank," which somehow felt much more appropriate.

When Papa Frank finally got on the line, an old and feeble voice, shaky with unshed tears, answered the phone. He was filled with questions he wanted to ask me and was overjoyed to have heard that Frank had had some happiness in the last months of his life.

When he learned that I had kids, he laughed at the thought that Frank was still trying to fulfill his father's deepest wish to become a grandpa. Frank's mother and brother had both died years before, and my Frank was his only remaining child.

Papa Frank hadn't known about me until he had learned about Frank's death, when he was told Frankie's girlfriend had been the one to place the call to the sheriff's office.

He told me how delighted he was to hear my voice and that I had called because he had no idea how to get in touch with me. He didn't know my name. He didn't have my phone number. He didn't know where I lived. For whatever reason, that information had never been passed on to him.

He had his friend, Palmer, take down my information so he could remember who I was and how to contact me. He would often tell me that no one was telling him what was going on. That he didn't know where Frankie was. That he didn't know what arrangements would be made for his burial, and that he felt so lost because, not only had he lost his child, but he'd lost control.

This man had run the family's business all his life. He'd started from a modest background and become a millionaire through hard effort, perseverance and concentration. He talked about how disappointed he felt that those were traits his son hadn't inherited and how hard it had been for them to connect at times. Then, he would share about how much he loved Frankie and was so sorry to see him gone.

He also admitted to me that, just a few months earlier, he had told Frank to take better care of himself; that at the rate Frank was going, if he didn't do something about his health and his diet soon, that he would outlive Frank. Oh! How he wished he wasn't right this time...

Our call lasted all of thirty minutes, when he became too tired to continue. As we concluded, I told him that I was supposed to be talking with the medical examiner's office again the next day and, if he wanted me to, I would call him afterward. He asked me to do that, and so we began a regular pattern of talking to each other just about every day. I made a point of making sure that, whatever questions he had, if I could answer them, I did. But, more importantly, in the days that followed, I realized this man mourned not only the loss of his son, but the relationship he had wished them to have.

Some of the stories he shared with me about Frank reflected his disappointment in Frank's choices in life. While I wanted to be Frank's defender in this, I realized Papa Frank just needed to talk. So, I curbed any response of leaping to Frank's defense in order to give Papa Frank the opportunity to share what it was he needed to say.

It wasn't easy, but it was necessary. I wasn't the only one grieving here, and we needed each other.

Digging Deeper...

Who else was impacted by the changes in your life? Whatever it is that happened, you can be certain you weren't the only one affected.

Sure, they may be impacted to a lesser extent than you, but the simple fact that there are people who love you means someone else's world was also shaken when this happened.

For me, it was my kids... I'd spent years making sure they felt safe and secure. They had a stable home life. We weren't rich, but they never went hungry. Despite my having to be both mother and father, they knew they were loved.

In the months immediately following Frank's death, I failed them in more ways than I care to think about. Their world was in chaos, and there was nothing they could do about it. The person they'd relied on for years for safety, security, stability and love had lost the ability to provide any of that.

The circumstances may be different for you, but it's important to remember that you're not the only one grieving and in pain. You're not the only one who is questioning all that they once held true.

Just as you need to experience that grief and pain so you can acknowledge it and move onward, others need to as well. And don't be surprised if their perception of the problem is unlike yours. They are viewing it from a different vantage point, and it will impact them differently. That's okay.

Part of the healing process is recognizing that pain is unique. What we mourn losing varies from person to person based on what had the most meaning to us. But recognize that you need each other as you take this *journey with grief. Isolation is the enemy now.*

IDENTIFYING FRANK

I had to call the medical examiner's office a few times over the days that followed before they had any new information for me. Identifying the body was proving difficult because of its condition. That was when I realized no one had told them about Frank's background. I shared with them how he had spent many years as an auxiliary state police officer for the state of Connecticut, stationed out of the Southbury barracks, and that he had a concealed carry permit for his beloved Beretta.

That was the information they needed to pursue things further on their end. However, they said it would take time, maybe even up to a week. The typical procedure was to fax the fingerprints to the FBI for a positive identification. Since Frank's body was so decomposed already, the quality of the print wasn't good enough to fax. They had to mail original copies of the fingerprint cards instead, and then await a response.

One thing I learned very quickly in working with the medical examiner's office is that what you see on TV dramas is nothing like real life. There is still a lot of manual work that goes into identifying a body, and the more manual work there is, the longer it's going to take.

Somehow, the idea of waiting another week before they potentially released his body was intolerable. It seemed to me there had to be something we could do to identify him sooner.

Since the dental records provided another avenue of identifying him, I began to pursue the information needed there, starting with the name of his dentist.

When I called Papa Frank that afternoon, I asked him if he knew the name of Frank's dentist. As far as he knew, Frank didn't have a dentist in Red Leaf, but he gave me the name of the family dentist they'd used here in Connecticut for years.

Thus, the rest of the day was spent on a dental record search. It turned out that the family dentist was no longer in business and had not been for a long time. So that was a dead end.

Months before, Frank had told me how to access his house in Connecticut because he'd asked me to do some checking up on it for him. I decided to go there to see if I couldn't find something that would give us a clue.

Frank was not the most organized person in the world under the best of circumstances. Given that he had been living in Florida for two and a half years, and since he had never intended to move down to Florida, there were certain things he hadn't gotten around to doing, like stopping his mail or having it forwarded. He hadn't even stopped his local newspaper. He'd been having a neighbor bring in his mail and his newspaper every day for two and a half years.

As I entered Frank's house, I spent more time wandering through it than I had in the past, trying to identify where he might keep his important papers. I anticipated maybe finding insurance papers or billing information or an address book where I could find what I was looking for.

After spending some time searching, I realized his pack-rat nature meant I could spend days going through things if I didn't come up with another solution. Having passed by the massive piles of mail sitting in his kitchen and overflowing into his living room, I realized my best chance was probably in finding a check-up reminder.

His neighbor told me a bit about the chronology of the mail piles, and I started with the most recent mail first, working my way backward until finally, I did find a reminder notice from his dentist. I called the medical examiner with that information before I even left Frank's house.

When they received the x-rays a couple of days later, they were old enough that it was difficult to get the match they were hoping for. However, by that time, the fingerprint identification finally came back from the FBI, positively identifying the body as Frank's.

All told, it took almost two weeks to make the identification before the body could be released to the funeral home.

Frank had told me about the family plot his father had purchased in Winter Park when Papa Frank and his mother had first moved to Florida. It was about three hours away from Red Leaf, where they subsequently moved. However, both Frank's mother and brother were already buried there, and Frank had anticipated eventually going there to bury his father too, never imagining he would be interred there first.

Due to the distance, it took the funeral home in Winter Park another week and a half before they were able to make the trip to pick up Frank's body. With the various delays, Frank's funeral was scheduled after Thanksgiving, a full month after he'd been discovered. The waiting had seemed unbearable. Yet, at least during that time, there were things I could do to keep busy. Little did I know, the funeral itself would pose its own problems...

MAKING ARRANGEMENTS

Papa Frank's affairs were handled by his financial advisor and trusted friend, Dan. During the course of my daily phone calls with Papa Frank, he told me that if I ever needed anything to let Dan know. When Papa Frank asked if I would be able to come down to Florida for the funeral, I told him that I hoped to, but was uncertain how I was going to pay for the airfare.

Without a moment's hesitation, Papa Frank told me he would have Dan make the arrangements. All he needed to know was that I was willing to come. He truly wanted to meet me. He had Palmer give me Dan's phone number to follow up and make arrangements for the trip.

We also had a long discussion about Frank's dogs. Falcore and Bear were brother and sister. They had never been apart. One of the things Frank and Papa Frank had argued about was Bear. Both of the puppies were born seemingly healthy, and Frank had found homes for all of the other puppies in the litter. However, Bear soon began to show symptoms that concerned Frank. By ten weeks old, it was clear that Bear was not a healthy pup.

Frank had already chosen Falcore as the puppy he wanted to keep from the litter, but he refused to saddle an adoptive family with Bear's medical condition and related expenses. As Bear grew, his back became misshapen, and one of his hind legs became useless.

Over the first year and a half of his life, Frank spent $10,000 trying to find a cure for Bear. After numerous surgeries and almost losing him once, Frank decided to let the poor pup be.

Despite Bear's deformity and handicap, he was a happy and loving dog. Yet, when Papa Frank looked at Bear, all he saw was imperfection. He assumed that with that amount of deformity, he must be in pain, and Papa Frank thought it was cruel not to have him put down.

As beautiful, intelligent and loving as Falcore was, Frank always loved the underdog. He would tell me sometimes, not to tell "the children," but he loved Bear best.

When Papa Frank and I discussed the future of the dogs and I told him I hoped to adopt them, he strongly encouraged me to take Falcore and have Bear put down. But knowing Frank's love for the dogs, I told him I wanted them both if he would let me have them.

I had already begun trying to find a way to transport them from Florida to Connecticut. I was researching a few nonprofit organizations that might help but was having little success in making arrangements. In the meantime, the poor dogs remained at the animal shelter.

I soon found that to be able to transport the dogs across state lines at all, I needed copies of their medical records. And thus began a whole new medical search. This time instead of seeking a dentist, I was seeking a veterinarian.

It took countless hours of research and calling, speaking with veterinary offices both in Connecticut and in Florida, but I finally found the veterinarian who had been seeing Frank's dogs. There was a catch though. According to Florida state law, the veterinarian could not speak with me about the dogs, their current condition, or provide any medical records for me until he saw Frank's death certificate.

Death certificates are issued by funeral homes, and only upon receipt of the body. So the holdup with the identification of Frank's body and the funeral home's delay in picking him up left the dogs in a state of limbo.

The animal shelter was not a boarding facility and was eager to have the dogs removed or destroyed to alleviate the burden on their overflowing facility. Yet, I couldn't move the dogs until I could prove my intent to adopt them (meaning they had to need a new owner).

Under the circumstances, the veterinarian was willing to work with me. While he couldn't provide me with any information about the dogs until I could prove ownership, he knew the dogs well, and he knew how much Frank loved them. Out of respect for Frank, he offered to board the dogs there until I could come up with the necessary paperwork. Since no other boarding facility would take them without proof of certain vaccinations, this truly was the only option I had.

THE BEST IS YET TO COME

As I got ready to go down to Florida for the funeral, I had no idea whether I'd be asked to say anything or not. In the interest of being prepared, and thinking it would just be his father and I representing the family at the event, I wrote a eulogy for Frank. In it, I shared all that Frank had come to mean to me, what I had learned about him both during our time together and in the intervening weeks since his death.

I concluded the eulogy with a story that Frank had shared with me, one of his favorite "re-senders."

> Frank once shared an email pass-along with me that he enjoyed. In it, a young woman was terminally ill. In meeting with her pastor, she told him of all the things she wanted for her service, which songs were to be sung and scriptures to be read.
>
> As he was preparing to leave, she stopped him and added that she wanted to be buried with a fork in her right hand. Puzzled, the pastor questioned why.
>
> She explained that as a child, she'd often been told at the end of special dinners to "keep her fork." It was always her favorite part because she knew that something better was coming… like velvety chocolate cake or deep-dish

apple pie, something wonderful and with substance.

In this story, she wanted people to wonder about the fork as they walked past her casket and for the pastor to share her story and remind them that *the best is yet to come*.

That's become my story now too. Frank's passing left a huge hole in my life. Never again will I listen to his voice as I drift off to sleep or hear it as I awake in the morning. There will be no more prayers together, notes that tease me, poems that please me, discussions that frustrate me, whining to irritate me, or projects that we share.

But as I mourn his loss, I recognize that I must also celebrate his life. His legacy isn't his death. His legacy is the lives he touched, the memories he created, and how he made people feel when he was with them.

That legacy isn't always rosy. There are many people he wasn't the kindest to, especially those taking care of his father. In hearing their stories, there were times I was ashamed of what he'd said and done.

Frank wasn't a perfect guy. Anyone who knew him knows that. He could be stubborn, ill-tempered and impatient at times, opinionated, outdated, belligerent, and many other adjectives I'm sure. He was a pack-rat extraordinaire, told bad jokes, and often crucified a good song with his own lyrics.

During his illness, he was unkind to me as well, sometimes irrationally so. I have since learned in speaking with medical professionals that his causticness in the last weeks was a symptom of his illness, a medical indicator that his diabetes was completely out of control. I knew it was not "in character" for the man I'd come to know in the months prior, and it was a relief to learn it wasn't him. At the same time, it made me feel badly that I hadn't pressed him more to seek medical attention earlier.

In reflecting on his legacy though, the less-than-stellar moments are outweighed by the countless acts of selflessness he performed. When Frank read about someone in need, he did everything he could to help. He gave money to buy what they needed. He paid utility bills to keep lights on, helped with back-payments so homes were saved from foreclosure. He bought food and clothing, donating them to help those in need. Frank even supplied pet food for those who needed it when they were in jeopardy of losing their animals. He always gave, not just at holidays, but year-round.

I've heard countless stories of people he helped, even to the extent that it left nothing remaining for him, and not just small sums too. When a friend needed to build a handicap ramp on her home for her recently disabled son, Frank provided the $15,000 that was needed.

I know some would ask why he kept giving when he'd tapped his financial reserves so much. Yes, some of it was due to poor decisions he made and people who took advantage of him. But I think the real answer lies in the values he held dear. When Frank was asked who the most influential person in his life was, he readily answered:

> That would have to be Jesus Christ. HE gave HIS life for our sins. HE taught us how to live in HIS image. HE taught us that the most important thing for us to be is our brother's keeper. WE are responsible for our fellow man.

Frank lived his life, doing his best to serve as his brother's keeper; not to judge or malign, but to help and aid those who needed it. He recognized that poverty is a man-made thing and, while he couldn't end it alone, he could make a difference in one person's life, and then another, and perhaps even another after that.

At his funeral, his aunt shared a story about a time when a neighbor's house caught on fire. While everyone was milling around afterward, trying to figure out what they could do to help, Frank was already in touch with the pharmacy, working on replacing the man's medications that had been lost in the fire, but that would be needed later that day. It may not have been the most urgent thing that needed doing, but it was a practical thing, and doing it was better than feeling helpless.

All of that is part of his legacy too.

Digging Deeper...

For the living, every loss marks a new beginning.

That can be a scary thing, especially if the ending of what we had wasn't of our choosing. Yet, even if it was our choice, the uncertainty of stepping out and starting something new can be intimidating.

The story of your life isn't always under your control. But how you react, what you let stop you... That is.

Will the devastating event you've experienced in your life stop you in your tracks? Will it keep you from living a life filled with happiness and purpose?

Or will you find that compelling reason deep within yourself to pick yourself back up, dust yourself off, and try again?

That job you lost isn't the only job in the world. That house that's no longer yours isn't your only chance for a home. That person you loved more than life itself wasn't your only reason for living.

Allowing any loss to keep you trapped in the past is depriving yourself and those around you of the future still awaiting you.

How much more damage will you allow that event to cause? Hasn't it already taken a big enough toll on your life?

Today. This day. You are still breathing. Take a deep breath. Feel the air fill your lungs. Now let it out. As your breath escapes your body, imagine the fear leaving with it.

What is one thing you can do right now to start moving forward? Today is a new beginning. Don't let the devastation this event has caused be the end of the story. It's in your power to create a new ending. What will it be? What legacy will you leave when you're done?

A PROTECTIVE FAMILY

During our talks, Papa Frank volunteered to pay for both my airfare and for transporting the dogs back home once we were able. He had more money than he was ever going to use, and he wanted to make things easier on me.

With his wife and children gone, the only family he had left was siblings and their children. When he died, the bulk of his estate was due to go to the community where he lived. His advisor, Dan, saw to any gifts and bequests he made, but when Papa Frank's family heard about me, I believe they became concerned about a perfect stranger coming into his life.

Without knowing me or understanding my motives, they rallied around him to protect him. They knew he wanted me to come down to Florida for the funeral and couldn't deny me that, but they made it extremely difficult for me to get there.

While Papa Frank had authorized Dan to arrange my transportation, including airfare, a rental car and lodging, the arrangements were never made. The date for Frank's funeral had been set, and forty-eight hours prior to it I still had no ticket. Through Dan, the family communicated to me that they didn't want me seeing Papa Frank while I was in Florida. There was to be both a graveside service at the cemetery and a memorial service in Red Leaf. I was told I was welcomed to the graveside service, but the memorial service would be a private event for family only.

It became clear that the only way my transportation arrangements were going to be made was if I agreed not to go to Red Leaf. Desperate to get there in time, I finally agreed. Unfortunately, we waited too long, and Dan wasn't able to make the arrangements.

Ultimately, I made the arrangements myself with only hours to spare. I would arrive in Florida at 1 a.m. on the day of Frank's funeral.

As I was packing for the trip, my friend, Larry, messaged me. We hadn't talked in a while and when he saw me online, he wrote to wish me a happy Thanksgiving and to see how I was doing. He knew nothing of Frank's death, and I shared with him what was going on in my life. It was then I remembered that this friend lived in the area I was going to. I asked him if he might have time to meet me the morning of the funeral so we could pray together for a bit.

At first, he responded that he wouldn't be able to get away from work, but as we chatted, he said to give him a few minutes and he would get back to me. The next thing I knew, we were making plans to meet at a local diner in the morning. He had invited another godly woman he knew and her husband to join us.

On the way to the airport, I called Papa Frank. I told him I was en route to Florida and would be at the graveside service, but his family was worried about his meeting me. I shed as positive a light as I possibly could on it, stating that they were concerned that seeing me would be too much for him.

It was the first time I'd ever heard Papa Frank angry. He demanded to know what it was that I wanted to do. I told him I wanted to see him. He said that was good because he wanted to see me too. Then he simply said in an exasperated tone of voice, "Do what you have to do!"

I spent the flight down to Florida and the three-hour drive from Jacksonville to Winter Park trying to figure out what it was that I had to do. I didn't want the family angry with me. I didn't want Papa Frank disappointed in me. I didn't want anyone thinking I was a gold digger. I didn't want to be attending my fiancé's funeral. Why did it all have to be so hard?

MY BREAKFAST MEETING

The next morning, I met Larry, Linda and her husband Len at a diner about five minutes away from the cemetery. Larry and I spent a few minutes catching up, talking about the trip down, and then the four of us just spent time talking. Larry, Linda and I all belong to a Christian writers' critique organization. At the time, Larry was president of the organization, and Linda and I were each chaplains of our respective chapters. So we talked about recent meetings, the writers we knew, and other things like that while we waited for breakfast to be served.

During breakfast, I shared a bit about the challenges of getting to Florida, the struggles I was having facing Frank's death, and the uncertainty I felt about the decision not to see Papa Frank. I still hadn't figured out what I had to do.

I'm not too certain how to describe this time together. While I knew I had Frank's funeral to attend in a couple of hours, there was something simple about meeting new people. I'm sure our common interests are what made it feel so natural.

As we finished our meals and the dishes were cleared away, that's when things started to get interesting. We had prayed together at the beginning of the meal and peace had descended on our table during our time together. It was clear that the conversation was now going to shift to deeper matters.

It still amazes me to this day, what the bonds of a shared faith can do. I had traveled hundreds of miles, left my home for a place I didn't want to come to, to participate in an event that I was afraid would break my heart.

I should have felt alone, but I didn't. As angry as I was with God and as hostile as I was feeling toward Him, I knew He had brought me to this place with these people, and that it was time for me to sit back and listen to what He had to say to me.

It was Len who started talking. He looked deep into my eyes from across the table and asked me a single question. "What can God do for you today?" He paused a moment to let the question sink in and then went on to say, "Before you answer, let me tell you a story about the last time I asked someone that question."

He went on to tell the story of a friend from church, who had been taking care of his father, who was dying of cancer. This friend was then diagnosed with cancer himself. Over the intervening months, while taking care of his father and undergoing his own chemo treatments, he became very ill. He lost significant amounts of weight and ultimately ended up in the hospital, a mere shadow of the man he had been.

Linda and Len went to visit this friend in the hospital. After talking and praying together for some time, Len asked this friend the same question he had just asked me. "What can God do for you today?" The man thought for a few moments.

When he answered, he said that he hoped God would grant him the strength to live long enough to take care of his father until his death. Given that he was at death's door himself, only a miracle could grant that desire. When Linda and Len left this friend's hospital bed, they fully expected it was the last time they were seeing him.

As the days passed and they heard no word of their friend's demise, they became curious. They called the hospital to ask what had become of him. When they were informed that he had been released, they were amazed.

It seems that in the days that followed since they last saw him, their friend had begun to rebound. He put on a little weight. He had regained some strength. He still had cancer. He was still going to die. But there was no reason to be kept in the hospital right then.

This man did go home and resumed his support and care of his father. When his father finally succumbed to his cancer, the friend died too a few short weeks later. Yet, the request he had made of God was answered, and he was at peace.

After sharing the story, Len looked at me again and said, "So let me ask you. What can God do for you today, knowing that the best is yet to come?"

I experienced two things at that exact moment.

One was the certain knowledge in the quiet of what was left of my heart, that the thing I wanted most was for God to allow me to see Papa Frank without causing a scene with his family.

The other was an excitement caused by Len's use of the phrase "the best is yet to come." It felt like the clearest affirmation I had ever received. I hadn't told Len anything about the pass-along Frank had sent, or that I had a printed copy of it with me at that exact moment in preparation for the funeral service.

These brothers and this sister in Christ earnestly prayed for me. They prayed that if seeing Papa Frank was part of God's will for my life, that all obstacles and barriers were removed, including my own fear. They prayed too for the healing of my heart and peace in my spirit. And for the first time in over a month, I felt a kernel of hope.

At other times in my life, I'd put my trust in the promise of Romans 8:28, that God would work all things together for good for those who love Him and are called according to His purpose.

Could it be that God could still make something good come from all of this pain? Was it possible, in my life, that the best really was yet to come?

As our time together drew to a close and the funeral hour approached, we finished our time in prayer. Other than my angry railing at God during the snowstorm, it was the first time I had spent in any form of significant prayer since Frank's death.

Digging Deeper...

Grief is a powerful emotion.

It can spawn feelings of anger, hatred, isolation, defeat, depression, powerlessness, shame, helplessness and so much more.

It can undermine all that you held true before it came into your life. It has the power to change your outlook on life, end marriages, trash careers, sever family ties, destroy faith, undermine confidence, and more.

Sometimes, we believe that the event that changed our lives was "done to us." There must be someone to blame. If we can't figure out who that is, it's easy enough to blame God.

We forget that there are natural ebbs and flows to life. People come into our lives, and they leave again. The longer we live, the longer the parade of people who pass through our lives becomes. No one is with us from beginning to end, except for God.

There are times when the best we can do is remind ourselves of what we believe.

I believe, without a doubt, that God works all things together for good for those who love Him and are called according to His purpose. (Romans 8:28)

Frank's death was the greatest blow I've ever suffered in my life. Would it have been better if we never met? I don't think so.

He would have died never knowing the love he so deeply desired. And when you love someone enough, putting their needs before your own is the right thing to do. Even knowing the outcome, I'd do it all over again.

In that, God gave us each a gift. He gave Frank someone to love and be loved by, and he gave me a lesson in His faithfulness. He never abandoned me in my grief, nor has He abandoned you. He will make something good come from this, if you let Him.

THE FUNERAL

As I left the diner and headed for the cemetery, I truly wished these people were coming with me. I had no idea how I was going to stand at the graveside service on my own, unwanted by Frank's family, feeling like an invader at my own fiancé's funeral.

I had arrived about twenty minutes before the service was to start. His coffin was already there. A few small rows of chairs standing in front of it. A bouquet of flowers on the ground nearby. A handful of people milling about. No one acknowledged my arrival.

As I stood before his steel grey coffin, I was struck by the fact that I was standing closer to him at that moment than I ever had before, and yet we were still so far apart. I wanted so much to see his face, to touch his hair, to know he was there. Yet, under the circumstances, it wasn't possible. Having traveled hundreds of miles, the journey somehow felt incomplete.

After standing and taking in the tableau for a few moments, I returned to my car feeling sick and discouraged. I sat in the driver's seat wondering if I had the courage and the strength to go through with this.

Suddenly another car arrived and parked a few spaces in front of me. A woman with short black hair got out, carrying a large, framed photograph in her arms. She walked up to the coffin, placed her hand gently upon it for a moment, and then set the photograph on the ground next to the flowers.

Up until this point in time, the only picture I'd seen of Frank was one that was more than ten years old, and a few others that he had taken in his bathroom mirror with his cell phone. They were blurry at best and fairly indistinguishable. He always intended to send me better pictures, but he never could figure out where his camera was. So it never happened.

As the woman (I later learned was named "Jane") stood up from placing the photo on the ground, she looked around and saw me in the car. Until now, I may as well have been invisible since nobody acknowledged me. As she drew nearer, I got out of my car. I could see she was carrying a photo envelope in her hand. She walked up to me and greeted me by saying, "You must be Tara. I heard that you didn't have any good pictures of Frank, and I thought you might like this one." The simplicity of the gesture and the kindness of the act brought a fresh wave of tears.

This was followed by an older gentleman who pulled a single red rose from the bouquet and walked up to me, saying, "I'm sure Frank would want you to have this."

With the ice broken, a few other people came and introduced themselves to me, but none of them from the family. There was a small group of people who had come for the occasion from the community where Papa Frank lived and a few longtime, local family friends in attendance. Frank's best friend in Florida, Wally, and his wife, Lori, had made the trip down too.

As the service began, it was as anticlimactic as you can imagine. The minister giving the message readily admitted that he didn't know Frank well. He shared a few stories of the brief encounters they had had and surmised what he could about Frank from them. He shared that he had no knowledge of Frank's spiritual state and so could offer no words of comfort or encouragement there. I've never attended a funeral like it before. It lasted all of ten minutes and then was over.

When Dan and I had spoken earlier about the plans for the day of the funeral, he had indicated that after the graveside service we would go out to lunch before making the long trip back to Red Leaf. As the funeral concluded and the handful of people there began to disperse, Dan and the family and pastor from Red Leaf drove away in the van without a word to me.

Jane recommended that Wally, Lori and I go to a local restaurant for lunch. Since I was still undecided about what to do after the service, I accepted the invitation. Imagine our surprise when we ran into the family at the restaurant!

They barely acknowledged our presence, quickly serving themselves from the buffet and leaving the restaurant as soon as possible afterward. The shortest distance from their table to the outside doors should have taken them right past our table. Yet, every single one of them went the long way around as if to avoid passing us by, including the pastor!

I was still wrestling with the question of whether to see Papa Frank or not. Even though it was what I had prayed God would make possible for me today, a few things would have to change to make that happen.

My original plan had been to drive up to Gainesville after the service, check into my hotel there, and await the arrival of a crate for the dogs that I was supposed to pick up the next morning at a local pet store. I finally had all of the paperwork necessary to be able to take the dogs home with me, even though I still had not met them. However, I needed an airline-approved kennel to be able to transport them. That had required special ordering and was due to arrive at the pet store the next morning.

If I were to change my plans so I could see Papa Frank, one of the things that was going to have to happen was that the crate would have to arrive early. Another was that my hotel would have to allow me to cancel without penalty so I could apply that night's room rate to a new hotel. Lastly, the Inn in Red Leaf would have to have room for me.

As we sat down to lunch, Jane asked me my plans for the rest of the day. I had already told her about the family's resistance to my meeting Papa Frank. She knew the family well and strongly encouraged me to go to Red Leaf, not just to meet Papa Frank, but to attend the memorial service the next morning. I told her that the family had said the memorial service was for family only and was private, but she told me she was going herself and had been invited, and knew it was open to the community.

Jane was heading to Red Leaf after lunch and called ahead to the Inn to make sure there was room for me. One of my three obstacles was covered. There was room at the Inn.

Having taken that first step, I called the pet store in Gainesville and learned they did have the crate in stock. Obstacle number two, destroyed.

To me, the most challenging one was to believe the hotel would allow me to cancel my reservation with less than 24 hours' notice without a penalty. Check-in time was only three hours away. But with the other two obstacles so easily handled, I called the hotel. I explained the situation to them and asked if it was possible to cancel without penalty. Under the circumstances, they gladly agreed with no argument at all. Obstacle number three, demolished.

Decision made. I was heading to Red Leaf and would meet Papa Frank. I would do what I had to do.

In Henry Blackaby's study, *Experiencing God*, one of the things he talks about is looking to see where God is at work, and then joining Him there. That's the sensation I had, seeing these obstacles fade away one at a time. Everything I had asked God to do for me that day seemed to be happening, and all I could do was join Him at work.

But before leaving Winter Park, there was one last thing I needed to do. After lunch, I asked Jane if she would show me the way back to the cemetery. When we got there, the chairs had been put away, the fake grass carpet rolled up and stored someplace, and all was quiet.

Jane waited at the cars as I took my Bible and stood by Frank's tomb. I needed for us to have one last Bible reading together; two chapters, one for me and one for him, just as we had always done it before.

I opened the Bible to where we left off. We had come full circle. Our next chapter was 1 Corinthians 12, the same chapter we had begun with when reading the Bible together. When we read, he usually read first. It seemed appropriate that the first chapter of our reading was the one that had answered his questions about spiritual gifts when we first started studying together.

The next chapter is known the world over, commonly read at wedding ceremonies, and rarely read at funerals, 1 Corinthians 13. The powerful verses about love are in this chapter, but the one that jumped out at me was verse 12. "For now we see only a reflection as in a mirror; then we shall see face to face. Now I know in part; then I shall know fully, even as I am fully known."

The only recent photos of Frank I had had until that day were reflections in a mirror, which made this verse very precious to me. In this world, all I ever saw was his reflection. But in the next, we shall see face to face. And as much as I tried to allow him to know the whole of me, he could never see it all. Yet now, I am fully known.

MEETING PAPA FRANK

After we left the cemetery, I followed Jane to Red Leaf and the community where Papa Frank lived. We checked into the Inn and went down to the cafeteria for dinner. After we ate, the moment I had been waiting for had arrived.

Jane and I drove to the building where Papa Frank lived. She asked me how I wanted to handle things, if she should go in first to let him know I was there or if I wanted to join her. We walked into his room together. He was sleepy at the time, but immediately perked up when he saw Jane.

Her father had been one of his most trusted employees for years. Frank and Jane had grown up together, and the families were close. Jane had been looking in on Papa Frank since the death of his wife, Jessie, four years earlier whenever she could make her way up to Red Leaf. She lived in the area around Winter Park where Frank was now buried alongside his mother and brother, Jeffrey, and regularly tended their graves.

When Papa Frank realized that Jane was not alone, his eyes drifted to me. I had sent him a card a few weeks earlier with a picture of me and the kids. It was sitting on his nightstand where he could see it. My hair was much shorter in the photograph I had sent, but I could see the dawning realization on his face that I had come. His eyes widened, his lips trembled, and his hand reached out for mine as he started to cry.

I think Jane recognized the need for Papa Frank and me to spend some time together alone because she soon found an errand to run, leaving us on our own. A week or two earlier, Papa Frank's friend, Palmer, had fallen off of a ladder and fractured his hip. So he was the newest resident of the nursing home. Jane decided she needed to go and see how he was doing.

Every day, Papa Frank watched the same video in his room, and he enjoyed sharing it with me that evening. He and Jessie had been avid square dancers, and he had a tape recording of the two of them dancing together that he watched repeatedly. He loved to watch her move and be reminded of her smile and see her sweet face.

He told me that as hard as it was to lose both of his sons, the death that he had the hardest time recovering from was the loss of his wife after sixty-three years of marriage. From the very first time he saw her at a dance just before shipping out for WWII, he knew he was going to marry her. They wrote letters to each other the entire time he was gone, and within a month of his return three years later they were married.

Unlike so many other people in my life, what Papa Frank was telling me with this story was that he understood. He knew what it was like for someone to become an inseparable part of your life in what seems like the blink of an eye. While he wished Frank had told him about me, he had no doubt we had something beautiful. He was amazed and pleased that I was going to marry Frank, and in the time that followed he made a point of letting everyone know I was Frank's intended.

In all honesty, having traveled that far, I really didn't feel a need to attend the memorial service. After the travesty of the graveside service, I was afraid of experiencing something similar the next day.

For me, the time I got to spend with Papa Frank that evening was enough. There was something I believed he needed to know, and I took the time to share it then.

I had listened to him talk in the weeks since Frank's death about the troubles between the two of them. Now it was time to make sure he knew how dear he was to Frank. I told him of our habit of prayer. I shared with him the things Frank had told me that he wanted to experience with his father and how much he loved him. I relayed the fact that there wasn't an evening Frank and I prayed together that we didn't pray for Papa Frank too.

When Papa Frank worried about Frank's spiritual state, I was able to reassure him. I told him about the time we had spent in Bible study and how precious our prayer sessions together had been to us both. I also told him about how Frank had thanked me for that time together and told me he felt closer to God at this point in his life than he ever had before.

When Jane returned to the room and we finished our conversation for the evening, Papa Frank asked if I would be at the memorial service the next day. I told him that I'd been told it was a private event for the family only, and I didn't want to intrude. He replied that I was Frank's family, and he wanted me there. So I promised him I would be.

Digging Deeper...

There are always two choices that lie before us, no matter what the circumstances. We can focus on ourselves or on others.

When we focus on ourselves, we start to see everything through the lens of our own wants and needs. Our grief tempts us to latch on to the loss we feel and hold on tight to it.

But that grief is an anchor and holding on to it will trap you in place.

Eventually, even if for moments at a time, lift your head and see the suffering of those around you. Remember... You're not the only one affected by your loss.

Talking; sharing stories, hopes and fears; trusting someone else with your innermost thoughts and feelings; and being there for someone else who needs the same. Thus begins the journey of recovery.

Healing starts when we can recognize the pain of another despite our own.

As time goes on, rest assured, you will be bowled over by fresh waves of grief. Grant yourself permission to mourn, to weep, and then to begin again. Always be kind to yourself in the process.

Whenever possible, seek to be an instrument in someone else's healing. As you step more outside of yourself and see the needs of others, healing comes, new purpose develops, and hope springs again.

THE SERVICE IN THE VILLAGE

I have to admit, there's not a lot I remember about the day of the memorial service. Jane had shown me around the village a little bit in the early morning, sharing stories she remembered of Papa Frank and Jessie and their time there together. She talked of the love they shared and how lonely Papa Frank had been since her death.

When we got to the chapel where the service was to be held, there were plenty of people from the community there already. Papa Frank was there with his sister and brother-in-law and their two sons. While I greeted him, it was easy to see he was a bit overwhelmed with all that was going on around him.

Eventually, the family all made their way up to the front pew to sit together. Jane joined them, but I had no idea what to do. There had been no invitation to sit with them, so I found a pew toward the back of the chapel and sat alone.

I wasn't alone for long. The director of the nursing home that Papa Frank lived in came and sat with me. We had met briefly the day before at the graveside funeral, and we exchanged a few polite words until the service started.

The same pastor who had given the message the day before, the one who admitted not knowing Frank at all, gave basically the same message again. He added in a few more stories he heard from others but gave little comfort or hope. This is what he had to say:

Some of his family members said this about Frank. If you were stuck on the side of the road, in the middle of the night, and pouring rain, while everyone else passed you by, Frank would be the one to stop and help you. This speaks volumes to me about a man I never really knew. He tells us what kind of heart he had.

Frank kept to himself most of the time. We all know he had his demons that he dealt with. I'm told though that he enjoyed times of prayer. The demons of our lives are oftentimes so strong that they overshadow the person we really are. And God forbid any of us are judged according to those things that easily entangle us. So today, we leave the judgment of Frank's salvation in God's hands.

There was a second man who officiated at the service as well. He was in charge of the music offerings and had a lovely singing voice. Frank would have approved. He loved music so much.

Although the service was longer than the one the day before, it seemed done and over within no time at all. Whereas the receiving line had been in the back of the chapel when I first came in, the family shifted to the front of the chapel to form a new line.

Uncertain what to do with myself, I went up to see Papa Frank. When he saw me, his hand reached for mine. He said, "I thought you didn't come." I assured him I had been there all along and had even said "hello" when I came in, but he hadn't noticed me at the time.

Either way, it didn't matter. I was there now. Papa Frank held my hand and wouldn't let go of it, so we greeted people together. With each new person who came to extend their condolences, Papa Frank would introduce me as Frank's intended with wonder and joy in his voice.

As people began filtering out of the chapel, the family gathered around Papa Frank. Plans were made for all of us to go to the cafeteria and have a meal together. Papa Frank insisted I sit by him, and we spent the rest of the afternoon together.

Despite the fact we had been talking together almost every day for the past month, it seems there was still so much to learn about one another and so little time to do it in. My flight home would leave the next day, and I still needed to gather up the dogs and prepare them for the long trip home.

It seemed that one part of my prayer had been answered. I had gotten to see and spend time with Papa Frank. Yet, it was still uncertain how much, if any, distress I had caused the family by coming. I seized an opportunity to spend a few minutes alone with Frank's cousin. I told him I wanted him to know that when I had said I wouldn't come to see Papa Frank I had meant it. I had had no intention of going back on my word when I gave it. I described Papa Frank's response when I told him I wasn't coming, and I told him it seemed much worse to put Papa Frank through that disappointment than it could possibly be for me to come and see him.

All the same, I wanted him to know I was sorry for any problems I may have caused within the family by showing up. He thanked me for my apology and acknowledged I had made the right decision. He could see how much having me there had meant to his uncle. The second part of my prayer had just been answered.

I left that evening to head to a town about an hour north to meet the dogs for the first time. I had no idea what to expect, but all I could think about was how Frank was supposed to be there. We often joked about blending our family together, wondering whose children were going to be more problematic, my two humans or his two canines. Never in my wildest dreams would I have thought I'd be finding out alone.

The flight back home was uneventful, despite having two doped-up, medium-sized dogs with me, but I was glad when the journey was over.

AN ETERNAL LOVE

Soon after I'd returned home from the funeral, I was sitting with my daughter, who was surfing YouTube looking for new popular songs she could learn. She loved sharing her favorites with me and asked if she could play me a new one. Although my heart wasn't in it at the time, I couldn't say "no." She needed my time and attention still, even if I struggled to feel connected with this world any longer.

She pulled up a music video of Christina Perri's "A Thousand Years," which had been written specifically for the soundtrack of the final segment of *The Twilight Saga, Breaking Dawn*. Thankfully though, I didn't know that at the time. (Frank would have found my selection for what I came to think of as "our song" to be hilarious, given that it was written for vampires!)

As the lyrics and music washed over me, I was drawn in by the sweet tones of the piano and strings, and then swallowed whole by the heart-wrenching confessions of the chorus. The lyrics built from their initial quiet strains and captured the pain and hope that filled my heart, culminating in the firm belief that time would bring the loved ones together and a promise of love everlasting.

I had waited for twelve years for Frank. I had prayed for ten years for the man God intended to be my husband.

It wasn't a thousand years, but it certainly felt like it when so many people around me were paired off, and I was raising children alone. It felt like I had waited forever to share my life with someone who loved me for me; not because of what I could do for them, but simply because I existed.

I was thoroughly convinced that God had created us for each other and had no doubt about it, which meant that in some ways, my heart had yearned for Frank since the beginning of time. I know that when we fully opened our hearts to each other, it felt like we'd known each other forever.

The song recalled for me the early days of our contact; the fleeting thoughts I had had. *Here was someone who seemed to like me. Could it be real? Or was it just a cruel joke?* Only time would tell. Yet, it didn't take much time at all... Not nearly as long as I thought it would.

Forcing myself to be brave, allowing myself to bask in new love again at my age and with my history and, suddenly, with one boldly written poem and an ensuing conversation, any walls I could have chosen to keep up came tumbling down. I was convinced they weren't needed with Frank. My heart was as precious to him as it was to me. For the first time in my life, I could trust someone else to enfold my heart in theirs and keep it safe and warm. No longer alone...

I had trusted God for the very best He had to offer me, believing all along that time would bring him to me. And He did. Frank was not a perfect person, and I would never argue that he was. But he was perfect for me.

A NEW BEGINNING FOR GRASSHOPPER

The month immediately following Frank's death was filled with so many activities. All of my time was spent dealing with the storm, handling Frank's affairs, and comforting Papa Frank. Very little time was left over for my children or my business.

In some ways, I was thankful for all the things that needed to be done. It gave me a reason to get out of bed every day, when I really had no desire to. I was even more thankful for a group of friends who had rallied around to take up a collection for me. It enabled me to pay most of my bills, despite the fact I hadn't been working.

Once I returned home from the funeral though, there was nothing left to do. Frank's estate was being handled by Papa Frank's advisor. The dogs were found and safely home. Frank's body was laid to rest.

With those tasks done, what was my life to be like? Five months earlier, that would have been an easy question to answer. However, Frank had come into my life and turned it completely upside down. Everything I looked at reminded me of him. The phone that we talked on, the laptop I wrote emails to him with, the dishes in the sink that I washed while he kept me company on the phone, the yard that needed raking, the dogs that needed exercising, the children that needed feeding and, more importantly, loving…

Each day dawned with a gaping void standing in front of me. I had no idea what to do with myself. I had no interest in work, or food, or seeing people, or in the fact that Christmas was right around the corner and, with it, my daughter's birthday.

I spent much of each day reading through Frank's emails and listening to voicemail messages he left for me and wondering how I was going to go on. It seemed unfathomable to me that, somehow, I was expected to live a life without him.

The pain of that time was intense. Without activities to keep me busy, it seemed all I had time for was to think. And when I thought, it hurt. I found myself experiencing such deep despair at times that all I could do was remind myself to breathe. To ask anything more of me would've been too much.

December 19, two months after our last conversation, would've been his sixty-first birthday. As the day loomed near, I found myself dreading it. It became a blot on the calendar that I wondered if I would survive. Realizing that the only thing that would get me through it was the prayer support of friends and family, I shared my fears with two dear friends.

On the day of his birthday, two deacons from my church called to ask if they could come to visit and pray with me. It was a loving and compassionate thing to do, and I was touched by their offer so I gave them permission to come.

Death is a strange thing though. There are no ready-made words that can comfort in every instance and curiosity can get the better of people. Once again, I shared the story of all that had been going on in my life. The response is what you would've expected, surprise that he died so young, frustration at his inability to seek medical attention because of lack of insurance, and pity for me for all I had lost.

While I was grateful for the intent that prompted their visit, by the time they left I felt worse than before. They had joined me in my grief, reminding me of the reason for its presence, when all I wanted was to escape from it.

A short time later my phone rang again. One of the friends I had confided in earlier called to see if she could stop by for just a few minutes. She didn't give any explanation why, but I agreed to let her come. About an hour later, there was a knock at my door.

I was amazed when I opened it to see her standing on my front porch, flowers in one hand and a cake in the other. I remember standing on the stairs looking at her in perplexity. I couldn't register what I was seeing, and I had no idea how to feel about it. But when I opened the door to let her in, she set down the cake and the flowers on the stairs so she could envelop me in her arms. A wave of understanding and gratitude washed over me.

We took everything into the kitchen and she pulled out some candles, put them on the cake, and lit them. Then we sang "Happy Birthday" to Frank. Tears choked back most of my singing, but she finished loud and strong. She instructed me to blow out the candles for Frank, which I did. She had even brought a card for him. In it, she talked about how glad she was that he'd come into my life and brought me such joy, and how much she looked forward to meeting him in Heaven one day.

The contrast between these two sets of visitors just a few hours apart was huge. The deacons, though well-intended, had done little to make me feel better. My friend, though outrageous, had made me remember that birthdays are a time to celebrate life. Rather than mourning my loss, together we celebrated the life Frank had lived and all that was good about it.

This day became the turning point for me. I realized I could spend my life focused on what I had lost, forgetting what it was that

I now had, or I could be thankful for the past and walk forward into the future. Thinking back to the story of the fork, I made a choice. Frank's pain and suffering were over. There were no more tears for him. For whatever reason, God wasn't done with me here yet.

I decided then and there that the only thing holding me back was the way I chose to view things. As long as I stayed focused on the loss, there was no way to celebrate life.

There were too many things Frank had wanted to experience with me. If I stayed anchored by my grief, life would pass me by. Then, at the end of my days, what would I say to him? Could I bear to tell him I'd given up on life because he wasn't there to share it with me? I can just hear him now! "What a waste! So much potential and so little accomplished. What were you thinking, Grasshopper?"

Digging Deeper...

Is it really as simple as making a choice?

For the most part, the answer is "yes." There are some extenuating circumstances when medical intercession may be needed, and you should consult with your doctor if you think this might be the case for you.

But for many people, happiness depends solely on where we choose to focus our attention.

Will we focus on what is no longer ours, or what someone else has done to us? Or will we embrace the possibilities of the future, the calling that pulls us to move forward? Can we find it within ourselves to be content with this moment and this hour?

In every day, there are challenges and there are blessings. Acknowledge the challenges, but don't fuel them with your energy. Focus your attention on the good things that come your way. Perhaps it's a beautiful sky, or the opportunity to take a walk, or that person who let you into busy traffic, or the chance to have lunch with a friend.

Challenge yourself at the end of each day to find three things that made you smile or feel grateful or feel loved.

Remember these things. Relive the warmth they made you feel. Surround yourself with people and circumstances that remind you you're alive and you're living a life worth living.

And if it's not quite the life you'd like to have yet, that's okay. You're a work in progress, just like me. Keep doing what you're good at, keep embracing the journey. As long as there is breath in your body, it's within your power to create the life you want to have.

The best is yet to come.

IN THE VALLEY

As hard as it was to go through losing Frank, it's amazing to look back and see how rarely I was alone. I struggled to feel God's presence. His comfort seemed non-existent. However, I came to trust that, despite our damaged connection, He was still very much involved in my life.

I began to see Him at work like the wind in the trees. You can't see the wind, but you can see the effect it has. I couldn't feel God's presence anymore, but I could see Him at work in the people around me. I could feel His comfort in the embrace of a friend.

That didn't change how alone I felt at the time! Yet, God continued to put people in my path to help, support and encourage me along the way. I only had to be willing to open my eyes and heart to see what He was doing.

It was at this time that I began struggling to reconcile all I had been through in the past few months. It seemed like such a harsh and cruel thing to put someone through and, if that's all it was for, then, yes, it was an awful thing for God to do to anyone.

Yet, the third verse of the hymn "How Firm a Foundation" gave a brief glimpse into another way to view the situation:

When through the deep waters I call thee to go,
The rivers of woe shall not thee overflow;

For I will be with thee, thy troubles to bless,
And sanctify to thee thy deepest distress.

Yes, I walked through the Valley of the Shadow of Death, and I survived. In time, the scorching I received there served to nourish me in ways that only trials can do. I could either choose to curse the time spent in the desert or be grateful for the lessons I learned while there. The choice was only mine to make.

When I considered what it would take to sanctify my deepest distress, I realized the only way I could potentially justify having my life completely upended in the span of four short months was if I allowed my pain and my experience to be used to help others. Without finding the good that could come from it, it was simply pain with no purpose, and I was determined not to let that be the case.

It was the only way I could find peace in my heart and mind about all I'd been through. That, and the notion that I had been the fulfillment of someone's deepest desire. I had been an answer to prayer. Frank had not died feeling alone in this world, even though at the moment of his death there was no one present with him. He knew, beyond the shadow of a doubt, that he was loved. That's the gift God used me to give to Frank.

THE IRONY OF PAIN

When we go through painful times in our lives, we often try to figure out how to avoid the pain as much as possible. We look for ways around it, hoping to skirt some of its effects. One of the many things I've learned from this whole experience is that there is no way around pain. It's a natural part of life.

The real trick to it is to learn how to go through pain. Yet, the only way through it is to step into it. You have to embrace it. You have to feel it in order to be able to acknowledge it, disarm it, and let it go.

There were other things I'd learned earlier in my life as I processed and recovered from the abuse and sexual molestation of my childhood. Pain and anger that's stuffed simply festers. It needs to be dealt with and addressed in healthy and safe ways.

It's also important to remember, everything that happens to us serves to mold and shape us. Many of the painful experiences I've had are things I never want to go through again. I'm sure the same is true with you.

Some of those experiences were the result of my own poor choices. Others were caused by the choices of others that I had no control over, but that had a direct impact on me and my life.

In both cases, I can choose to view them through the eyes of a victim or a victor.

As a victim, those experiences trap me and weigh me down, making it impossible to move forward without carrying them along with me like so much excess baggage. They anchor my life in those experiences, limiting the possibilities for my life as I live it now.

As a victor, I can acknowledge those experiences, accept responsibility where needed, and allow my response to mold and shape me into the person I want to become. This approach allows me to even reach a point of gratitude for painful experiences because they make me who I am today. And when I'm living life as a victor instead of a victim, there's great freedom in that.

However, it had been so long since those early experiences that I'd forgotten the irony of pain. As much as we want to avoid it, the only way to deal with it is to experience it.

Our tendency to avoid painful things is because we don't want to be in that place. We don't want to be hurt. We don't want to endure what it is that we're being asked to endure, whether by circumstances beyond our control or by circumstances we've created ourselves.

The only way to actually healthily get through emotional pain is to step into it. Be true to who you are. Acknowledge how it makes you feel. Don't try to avoid or hide from the pain, because it's only going to linger there waiting for you to deal with it later on, and it will rear its ugly head at the most unpredictable of times.

In Isaiah 42:3a it says "A bruised reed he will not break, and a smoldering wick he will not snuff out." When we are in pain, we are like that bruised reed. The wind buffets you around and makes you sway and bend. It may even seem like more than you can handle, like it's going to completely flatten you. Remember though that God has a plan for you, and that plan is not to harm you, but to grow you and prosper you. (Jer. 29:11)

Any athlete knows you have to be active. You have to move in order to grow stronger. If you stand still, you weaken and atrophy.

So, the winds God sends to buffet you are intended to make you stronger. He knows your limits, even more than you do. He will sanctify your deepest distress if you let Him.

As a martial artist, I've found many times I've been surprised at how much more I can do than I thought I could. We are our own worst enemies when it comes to our limitations because we set the bar to a point where it's still comfortable, when in actuality we can push farther out of our comfort zone and into an area where true growth can happen.

Perhaps you're in pain right now. As with all pain, I know you would much prefer not to go through it. During the events of this story, I honestly saw no way I could survive what I was going through. There were moments when I had to remind myself to breathe and that was the most I could expect of myself, and even that was painful to do. But I can tell you I have become stronger and more fully the person God designed me to be by being open to another human being, even at the risk of experiencing pain.

Sometimes they say, if a bone that's been broken sets incorrectly, the only thing you can do is break it again so it can be set properly. With the dysfunction I grew up with, my spirit was that broken bone. When I healed in such a way that I couldn't connect with people, not deeply and not truly, I always had to keep my guard up. I had to keep myself safe from harm.

It took many years of being alone after being re-broken and set properly by God before I was strong enough to even contemplate letting somebody back into my life. And I was thoroughly amazed how much stronger and healthier and God-centered my life could be than it ever had been before.

So when you experience pain, think of this time in your life as a time when God is working in you. Don't try to avoid the pain or hide from the world. Experience what it is that's happening in your life to the degree you can at the time and know you are not alone as you go through it.

I'm not saying be wide open to pain, but I'm saying that, as you're able, take it out, feel it, acknowledge it. Little by little, you will work your way through this, and you have two choices in doing that.

The choice is yours. Will you come out with a deeper understanding of God and the possibilities for your life or will you come out more isolated and alone than you've ever been before? Those are the two choices. I hope you choose God.

Digging Deeper...

Are you a victim or a victor?

A victim says, "this happened to me, and I'm helpless to change it."

A victor says, "this happened to me, and I can't change the past, but the future is mine to make."

Life is hard. There are no two ways about it. There will be challenges and struggles, both big and small.

But even the bad times in our lives can serve us. They can teach us patience and empathy. They can help us relate better to others with similar stories. They can serve to remind us of the choices we want to make and the things we want to do with our lives. They can help us to clarify our purpose and vision.

Pain is never fun. Yet, without it, we can't grow.

How many trials have you been through in your life that only served to make you who you are today?

Circumstances mold and shape us every day. It's how we choose to respond to those situations and what we do with them that counts.

Being a victor only takes getting up one more time than you're knocked down.

Don't let anything keep you from getting back up and making the difference in our world you were born to make.

THE GIFT FRANK LEFT BEHIND

I've often thought about the kind of legacy I want to leave behind when I'm gone. I've attended the funerals of friends where the service was packed, and others were there were few in attendance. I can't tell you how many times I walked away from a funeral hearing stories about a person I thought I knew well, only to have learned new things about them from others. There's a certain satisfaction in hearing stories about a loved one that you hadn't heard before. It keeps them alive.

When my time comes, I hope my funeral is one of those that's packed with people who knew me, who felt they were special to me and yet find new stories to hear from others who knew me too.

After Frank's death, I continued to hear stories about him; some from people who knew him well, and others who had only known him online or over the phone. Yet, he touched countless lives over the years.

I think the life he changed most profoundly was mine though. The person I was before he came into my life was content and doing alright in her life, without realizing she was living smack-dab in the middle of her comfort zone.

When I made the decision to share myself fully with Frank, with no walls for a barrier or protection, I allowed myself to be wholly loved by someone else for the first time in my life. I hid nothing. I was 100% truly and authentically myself. My flaws and insecurities were plain to see, and he loved me anyway.

His loss left me too shaken to even begin to figure out how to put walls back up. They would have been too little, too late, even if I had. So, the people who reached out to me, to comfort me and mourn with me, saw me in my most vulnerable state, and I really didn't care.

As I began to heal after making the decision to celebrate life rather than staying focused on loss, I found I had no desire to hide my vulnerability any longer. Too many people were responding to it, recognizing the same thing in themselves, and appreciating having someone be so transparent about it.

I realized the more I allowed people to see what I was going through, the more authentic I was being to myself. And the more I lived my life as my authentic self, the more peace I felt.

I wasn't trying to impress anyone or get anyone's attention. I was simply permitting myself to be who God created me to be. The more I centered myself on that, the stronger and more capable I felt. I'd spent years hiding behind my walls, preventing myself from using my gifts and talents fully, because I might get hurt, or I might not be accepted, or I might not succeed.

So, the greatest legacy Frank left me was the permission I hadn't given myself before; the permission to fully be me. It took his loss, ultimately, for me to become whole again.

A NEW BEGINNING

If the story were to end there, God would be good even if Frank and I only had four months together and never did actually get to meet in person.

That statement may feel more comfortable to you if I wrote instead that "Life would be good..." Regardless of your theological perspective, life is made up of a series of contrasts. We can only truly know one thing when it's compared to another (or a lack of another). We know hunger because we know satisfaction. We know light because we know dark. We know comfort because we know need. And I believe we cannot fully experience joy without knowing pain.

I was blessed to be the answer to Frank's prayer to find his last relationship. That remains a precious gift to me to this day. It fills my heart to think that my love, my time, and my attention were a blessing to him in his last days and that I was an answered prayer.

Not only that, but Frank met my deepest desire to be loved completely for myself alone. There were no conditions and no boundaries to our love for each other. Perhaps, in the end, that wasn't a sustainable relationship here on Earth. But for a moment in time, I was the whole world to someone else. Frank filled my hunger to belong and made me feel wanted. For someone who spent all of her life looking for a place to fit in, that was no small feat.

On the day of Frank's birthday celebration, I realized I could continue to mourn the loss of all of that, or I could be thankful I'd had it at all. If I continued to mourn, I'd be stuck in that space, unable to move forward, unable to heal.

Not to say that mourning doesn't serve a purpose. It does! And it shouldn't be rushed. But anyone who has ever lost something or someone precious to them knows, there comes a time when mourning is no longer serving you. You start to serve it.

That's when you have to start turning your face in another direction and seeing what it is that you've been missing while mourning. That's when you start to see who has joined you in the Valley, to uphold and sustain you as you walked through that difficult place and time in your life.

On Frank's birthday, I decided it was time to pick my life back up again and figure out what could still be made of it. I gave myself until the first of the year to settle into the idea and to regain my bearings, not as a New Year's resolution, but because it was a good time for a new start. In the year since then, so many milestones were reached and he's been a part of each of them.

In April, I went to Philadelphia and tested for my black belt; just as Frank wanted me to do. I took his photograph with me as I made the four-hour drive and talked with him most of the way there.

When I'd first found out in class on May 8 that I'd passed my test, I was thrilled! Yet, on the ride home, I started to feel the remorse of Frank not being there. Not only that, his father had died two days earlier on May 6. For many months, when there was something I wanted to share with Frank, I called Papa Frank and shared it with him instead. Suddenly, I was faced with no one to connect me to Frank anymore.

Driving home, I burst into tears again. When I got home, I got online and the first thing I saw was that a music group I like, The

Piano Guys, had posted a new video, unannounced. Normally, they combine a contemporary piece with a classical piece, making a new arrangement that's fresh and unique. This time, it was just one song. Wanna guess which one? "A Thousand Years."

A fresh wave of tears swept over me, yet this time it wasn't grief, but shame that I'd doubted my Father's love. This unexpected gift from God reminded me that Frank will always be near me since I carry him with me in my heart.

A month later, I made the trip back to Philadelphia to attend my promotion ceremony and officially became a black belt in the World Tang Soo Do Association. Frank had wanted to attend both the test and the promotion ceremony with me. They were milestones in my life that he was proud of.

The final milestone Frank wanted to share happened in September that year. The book I'd been co-authoring when Frank and I first connected was finally released. *The Character-Based Leader* is making a difference in people's lives, and Frank is a small part of its legacy.

The day I held a copy of it in my hand was another turning point for me. As excited and giddy as I was to know it was finally published, it also represented the last milestone Frank and I had discussed sharing, other than our wedding, which we'd planned for the summer of 2013. There was nothing left to look forward to.

Suddenly, this exciting time became a solemn one. Some form of observance and celebration was required. But what? I was home alone when the books arrived. The kids were at school. My Mom was at work.

I realized there was one final thing Frank and I had planned to do together. There was a restaurant we were going to go to on our first date.

Since he never made it back to Connecticut, we never went on that date, and I'd avoided the restaurant since; initially, in anticipation of our time together and ultimately because I couldn't bear the thought of going without him.

Yet, God has a sense of humor… Frank always assured me of that.

A couple of months earlier, I met a man at a local business event. There was something about him that drew me in and stirred my interest enough that I looked forward to getting to know him better and sought out ways to do so.

As opportunities presented themselves, I stepped out in faith, following God's leading. We spent some time together, no pressure, just business at first, then a little bit of socializing. A friendship has grown there that was totally unexpected and truly a blessing.

For me, things changed completely the day the book arrived. I called my new friend and told him it was here, and how it was the final milestone with Frank and the sadness that went along with that. I also told him I wanted to go out and celebrate and how I had settled on what I wanted to do. I went out on a limb and asked him to come with me, and he accepted.

That evening was a perfect blend of completion with Frank and possibilities for the future; an ending and a beginning in complete synchronicity.

I expected the evening to be haunted by the memory of Frank, and yet it was filled with the gentle kindness of my friend, a man so different from Frank in many ways, yet appealing to me all the same. I thought I might shed a few tears. Instead, I laughed.

Frank will always be a part of me, as well as of my future. But Frank's work in my life is done. It's taken a year, but there's nothing new left for us. My hand has been passed from one love to embracing the possibility of another, whether with my new friend or ultimately with someone else, I don't know, but I'm amazed by God's goodness to me. The heart that I thought was shattered forever still beats, and hopes.

If anyone had told me a year ago that I'd feel love again one day, I never would have believed them, and while this new relationship may never develop into anything more than it is today, I'm not willing to close myself off from it.

As Frank taught me, when God's leading the way, the best is yet to come...

AUTHOR'S NOTE

Over the years of my Christian walk, there have been many things I've learned as I've read and studied the Bible. It's amazed me how verses take on new meaning when circumstances in my life change. When I first came to faith, Philippians 4:13 was crucial to me. Later on, Romans 8:28 came to have beautiful significance to me, reminding me that no matter how much I had messed up my life, God could still make something good out of it.

Eventually, Psalm 139 came to have precious meaning to me as well, as I awaited the birth of my son. But as I think back on the year after Frank's death, I think one of the most beautiful passages is the simplest. "Jesus wept." (John 11:35)

Jesus wept at a time when he had heard about the death of his friend, Lazarus, even though he knew he could raise Lazarus to life everlasting. Why did he weep?

I think he wept because when we meet another person soul-to-soul, we become crucial parts of each other. Even knowing that the time of parting was short and wouldn't last forever didn't take away the crushing blow of Lazarus's death for Jesus. And for those who are grieving, that should bring comfort.

One of the things so many people who are grieving deal with is the idea that it should only last for a time. Or that there is a certain prescribed manner in which it's okay to grieve. The problem is, that's just not the case. We each grieve in different ways. We each have different needs during that time. And it will last different lengths of time for each of us.

I was surprised in a recent conversation with a friend of mine who has been mourning the death of her son for the last three years, when she talked about the fact that it's something she just can't move on from. Frank's been gone for a little over a year now, and I've moved on in a variety of ways.

It doesn't mean that Frank's place in my life has any less significance or any less of an impact. What we had is something I'll cherish forever. And I do look forward to the day when I finally get to see him. But, if I stay stuck in the grief and stuck in the mourning, I miss the beauty of this day because I'm clinging to yesterday. And in the beauty of this day, I have friends and opportunities and a family, people who love me and people who want to see me succeed.

If I'm chained to the past, I can't move forward. And if I can't move forward, there's no new success. There's no new opportunity. There's no new life, and there's really no future potential for happiness because I've deprived myself of living today.

That doesn't mean that we shouldn't weep or we shouldn't mourn. I think that's something we need to fully embrace. We need to fully experience it. We need to go down into the depths of the pain and acknowledge its existence. And I think we even need to periodically revisit it, as I have while writing this book.

What I've found is that the depths of pain change over time. How deeply we can go into it and how much we can allow it to touch our lives changes based on how sore we are at the time, how lost we feel, and how crushed we are.

As I've begun to heal and embrace my life again, what I've found is that I can go a little deeper into that grief. I can acknowledge a little bit more of that loss and pain, as well as the significance it had and the things I felt robbed of in losing Frank.

I think it's important to do that, because it's only in acknowledging what we think we have lost that we can turn to God and say, "thank you for what I had" and "thank you for whatever it is you have planned for me."

As Jeremiah reminds us in 29:11, God does have a plan and a purpose for us, and it's not to harm us. Pain will come into our lives just as it did in Jesus's. Yet, that's not where He intends to leave us.

Jesus wept for the loss of his friend. Have you ever wondered why? He knew Lazarus was with the Father. There was no pain, or sickness, or trial. He was in Heaven, experiencing perfect life and perfect love.

A friend has suggested that perhaps Jesus wept because he knew he was going to have to take Lazarus back from all of that. I think it's more though. Jesus took on human form to fully experience the human condition. He didn't hold himself back from any of the hardships we endure. I believe Jesus wept in pure, unadulterated grief because he chose to experience the same pain that I have experienced.

Perhaps he even felt betrayed for a moment by his Father, just as I felt betrayed by God, thinking that He'd dangled the thing I wanted most in front of me and snatched it away at the last minute just before I was able to grasp it. We'll never know on this side of the veil, but it's one of those questions I look forward to having answered someday.

In the meantime, I still yearn for that person in my life that I can share every day with. I have friends who fill in the gaps for now, but the thing is, it's all in God's time. When I have lived my life according to God's plan for me, I know my heavenly Father just wants to give me the best of life. And so, I've learned to wait on Him. I haven't learned to be patient yet, but I'm learning to be content.

I'm beginning to see that I had erected walls around my heart and my life that would still be keeping people out to this day if Frank hadn't taken them down. It's because Frank came into my life at the time he did and I chose to experience fully what was being offered to me that my heart is open now. So, perhaps, the purpose of Frank wasn't to be "The One" for me but to prepare me for The One to come. Only time will tell...

Certainly, the list of qualities I'm looking for in an ideal partner has changed. It's grown and adapted based on things I learned in my relationship with Frank as well as over my years spent alone.

Frank was the fulfillment of the first list, and no one will ever take his place. But one thing I've learned in having this new friend come into my life is that loving a partner is very much like loving your kids. When the second one is on its way, it's easy to wonder how you will ever be able to care for them as much as you do the first. Yet, the human heart is meant to infinitely expand. When love is pure, there is always room for more.

And so, I am at peace with God's will in my life, whatever that might be. It allows me to have hope for the future, knowing my Abba, my Daddy, loves me dearly.

Thank you for reading *The Best is Yet to Come*. My hope is that my story and the lessons I learned will help others to process their own grief. If that is accomplished, this will all have been worth it. But I need your help to reach those who need it most. Your review is crucial for new readers to determine whether this book is right for them or not. So, if you've enjoyed reading it, please leave a review on your favorite review site.

DISCUSSION GUIDE

Three sets of discussion questions follow. Two are for book clubs (one secular, the other Christian) and the third is for grief support groups. I hope you and your group find these helpful as you dig deeper into *The Best is Yet to Come*.

Book Club Discussion Questions

1. What was your favorite part of the book?

2. What was your least favorite?

3. Did you race to the end, or was it more of a slow burn?

4. Which scene has stuck with you the most?

5. What did you think of the writing? Are there any stand-out sentences?

6. Did you reread any passages? If so, which ones?

7. Did reading the book change your perspective or make you reflect on your own life? If yes, how?

8. What surprised you most about the book?

9. How realistic do you think it is to develop a deep relationship with someone you've never met in person?

10. If you could ask the author anything, what would it be?

11. What do you think of the book's title? How does it relate to the book's contents? What other title might you choose?

12. Did this book remind you of any other books? If so, how did it compare?

13. If you were making a movie of this book, who would you cast?

14. How did the author's story impact you? Do you think you'll remember it in a few months or years?

15. Would you ever consider re-reading this book? Why or why not?

16. Do you think the author succeeded in what they set out to do in writing this book?

17. What is the most important point the author makes in this book?

18. Are there lingering questions from the book you're still thinking about?

19. Would you recommend this book to a friend?

Christian Book Club Discussion Questions

1. What areas of Christianity did this book highlight or tackle? Was it done successfully?

2. What is the central message of this book? Share a passage that highlights this message.

3. Have you ever shared your faith in a way that you anticipated someone would reject, only to find out they held the same beliefs?

4. What did you think about Nigel's advice regarding making a list of the characteristics your ideal partner would have?

5. Do you think it's okay to be light-hearted and joke with God in prayer?

6. Do you believe in spiritual warfare? If yes, can you give an example of a time you've experienced it?

7. Have you ever tested God to determine his will, like when Tara gave God the three tasks to do if she was supposed to visit Papa Frank?

8. Do you think it is ever a mistake to pray for patience?

9. What did you think of the story about the woman wanting to be buried holding a fork?

10. Have you ever considered what type of legacy you'd like to leave behind?

11. Were you surprised by how different the visits from the deacons and Tara's friend on Frank's birthday felt?

12. Do you think it was wrong for Tara to be angry with God?

13. Do you believe God ever gives us more than we can handle?

14. Is faith a muscle? The more we exercise it, the stronger it grows?

15. Is being a victim or victor simply a matter of perspective?

16. How do you feel about what the author experienced?

17. Are you inspired to do something after this reading? Explain.

18. Do you feel that your own faith has grown or changed by what you read in this book?

19. How can you put the lessons of this book to work in your spiritual life?

20. Is any of the material in this book controversial? Why or why not?

21. What is your overall impression of the author?

22. What can God do for you today?

Grief Support Group Discussion Questions

1. Have you ever wanted a specific outcome so much that you almost missed seeing the good that came out of not getting what you wanted?

2. What did you learn when that happened?

3. How well do you think you compromise with others?

4. What makes it easier for you to compromise?

5. Do you find that others typically understand what you want? If yes, how do you know?

6. How do you react when things don't go according to plan? Are you disappointed or do you look for the good in it?

7. How comfortable are you with being vulnerable with the people closest to you?

8. How comfortable are you with being vulnerable with strangers?

9. Do you enjoy being challenged by others to try new things?

10. How do you handle confrontation?

11. Are there things you wish you did differently during confrontations? If yes, what? And why do you think that would better?

12. Do you find you can get stuck on what you've lost, rather than appreciating what you had?

13. What would it take to change your perspective?

14. We all have lost things in our lives; some were minor and others were life-changing. What was the most devastating loss you've been through thus far?

15. How long ago did it happen?

16. How did you respond to it at the time?

17. How do you feel about it now?

18. Who else was impacted by that loss?

19. How did they respond to it?

20. Did you find their response helpful?

21. In hindsight, what do you wish you'd done differently?

22. Do you feel anchored in the past by this event?

23. What do you think would help you get "unstuck" again?

24. Are you good about permitting yourself to grieve?

25. How can you reframe your perspective of your loss in a more positive light?

26. What's one thing you can do right now to start moving forward?

ACKNOWLEDGMENTS

Where to start? There are so many people who had a hand in bringing this book to light.

Thanks to the Word Weavers Berkshires group for your encouragement, critiquing and support as I got started on this book. Carol Barnier, you've been the voice of experience and reason for me. Your guidance and early input have been invaluable to me, as has your friendship. I'm truly grateful. And to James Early, my editor, thank you for having the courage and integrity to point out problem areas in the story. The resulting work is much better, thanks to you.

I'm grateful too for the Lead Change Group led by Mike Henry, Sr. You rallied around me when I needed you most, despite never having met in person before. You'll never know how much your support, love and care mean to me. It transcended the bonds of our virtual connection and had a deep and lasting impact on me. Special thanks to Chery Gegelman, who made it a point to reach out, stay in touch, and support, listen, pray for, encourage and remind me I wasn't alone. Consider yourself hugged, lady!

To Larry Leech and Linda and Len Lisak, thank you for making a stranger feel like family, and standing by me when I needed it the most.

Cyndi Nisly, you reminded me that it's more important to celebrate life than to live in the past. Thank you for bringing the party to me when I couldn't come to the party. I think it's time for chocolate cake!

To my instructors and friends at Northern Star Karate, what can I say except thank you for giving me the extra push I needed to get back on my feet again. Tang Soo! I'm especially grateful for Al Thierfelder, who simply understood. Your words during my black belt promotion ceremony have lingered with me, Sir. Thank you for being sensitive to the deeper significance of that day for me. I couldn't have asked for a better teacher, encourager or friend.

Thanks too to Jill Thompson for reminding me every week that God could handle my anger, as well as everything else I was and wasn't feeling. Having you walk with me through this journey of faith has been one of God's greatest blessings to me.

To my sister, Rachel Dickinson, and her husband, Brian, I pray that you have many happy and healthy years together. While we each became engaged around the same time, you've been able to fulfill that promise to one another. May you continue to be kind and caring toward each other, and experience a lifetime of love together.

As for my children, Eliza and Timothy, I'm so very proud to be your mother, and I'm sorry for the pain I put you through as you watched my life (and as a result, your own) spiral out of control. I know I can't ever make it up to you, but know that I love you both, beyond measure. Always remember... I'll love you forever, and I'll like you for always.

To my father, Enoch Alemany, thank you for your love and support. It still warms me to think of the phone call when I first told you about Frank. Your first question was whether or not you'd be able to intimidate him, because that's what fathers do. Seems we'll have to wait a bit longer to find out the answer to that one, but thank you for reminding me that I'm your little girl, no matter how old I get.

Acknowledgments

Lastly, there is one who tilled the soil of my life, planting seeds that took root in God's time. You never gave up, despite my repeated rejections of what you had to offer. Thanks, Mom! You are precious to me, Christine Freeman. I can't say where I'd be today without your example as a Christ-follower who demonstrates what faith is all about while walking the little way. I certainly would never have endured the painful experiences laid out in this story without the steadfast love of my Lord and Savior Jesus Christ, to whom you introduced me.

ABOUT THE AUTHOR

Tara Alemany defies a simple definition. She is a multi-award-winning author of seven books. She is also a speaker, business consultant and publisher.

She founded her publishing company Emerald Lake Books in 2014, which she co-owns with her best friend, Mark Gerber. Their boutique publishing company provides a unique blend of business coaching with publishing to help its authors succeed, whether it's their first book or their fiftieth!

Tara's latest award-winning book, *Publish with Purpose*, reveals the unique process developed by Emerald Lake Books to help their authors set and attain their goals.

In addition to publishing, consulting, writing and speaking, Tara serves on the Board of Directors for a Christian writers' critique group, acting as both president and chaplain of the group. In her spare time, she is a winemaker, a military Mom to two young adults (one of each), and is owned by a black cat.

If you're interested in having Tara speak to your group or organization, you can contact her at emeraldlakebooks.com/alemany.

For more great books, please visit us at
emeraldlakebooks.com.

Sherman, Connecticut

www.ingramcontent.com/pod-product-compliance
Lightning Source LLC
Chambersburg PA
CBHW030151100526
44592CB00009B/224